MARRIAGE AND DEATH NOTICES FROM
PENDLETON (S. C.) *MESSENGER*
1807–1851

Please Direct All Correspondence and Book Orders to:

Southern Historical Press, Inc.
PO Box 1267
375 West Broad Street
Greenville, SC 29602-1267
or
southernhistoricalpress@gmail.com

----

southernhistoricalpress.com

ISBN #0-89308-049-7

The Pendleton Messenger was the first newspaper in the Up-Country of South Carolina, having its beginning in 1807. It was printed in the town of Pendleton, which was the seat of Pendleton District. That district was abolished in 1828 to form Anderson and Pickens districts, and it encompassed the present counties of Anderson, Pickens, and Oconee. These marriage and death notices are from the entire state. For the reason already stated, the up-country was covered. However, low-country notices also appeared in this paper, because it was a favorite summer residence of many persons from Charleston and Georgetown, and some of them made Pendleton their permanent home. Also, the first editor, John Miller, had resided in Charleston himself. Pendleton District bordered in North Carolina and Georgia, and frequent notices are from the border counties of those states. The exact date of the demise of the Pendleton Messenger. The last extant issue is from 1851, but the paper was still in operation as late as 1859.

Some thirty years ago, Professor J. M. Lesesne abstracted marriage and death notices from this paper, and contributed them to the South Carolina Historical and Genealogical Magazine. Professor Lesesne carried them only through 1823. For convenience and because some issues are now available which Professor Lesesne did not have, I have re-abstracted the notices for those years, and all subsequent extant issues. All the issues which are abstracted here can be seen either originals or on microfilm at the South Caroliniana Library, Columbia, S. C., with the exception of June 17, 1818-May 12, 1819 and December 27, 1844 and February 7-28, 1845 which are at Clemson University. Many issues contained no marriage or death notices; therefore, the files are actually more nearly complete than these abstracts will show.

My thanks go to the South Caroliniana Library for their cooperation and to Miss Karon Mac Smith for her fine job in indexing.

Brent H. Holcomb, C. R. S.
Clinton, South Carolina
September 20, 1976

Issue of March 20, 1807 (Vol. I, No. 10)
Died in Charleston on Monday, 2d inst., Mr. William M'Kimmy, in the 20th year of his age. He turned out in one of the Beat Companies, at the Brigade Review, on the 23d ult., and not having provided himself with a box for his cartridges, he deposited them in his waistcoat or breeches pocket to which the flash from his pan communicated as he incautiously fired his piece, and he was shockingly burnt: He languished in great agony till his death.

Issue of March 27, 1807
Married on Tuesday 17th, Mr. Rhodam Doyle to Miss Jane Bruster, daughter of the late Mr. James Bruster of this District.
Marries, Mr. Benjamin Armstrong to Miss Sally Neiley, both of this District.

Issue of April 3, 1807
Died at Greenville Court House, on Tuesday last suddenly, Dr. William Handworks, for several years a practitioner at that place.

Issue of April 17, 1807
Married on Thursday 9th inst., Mr. Lewis Barton, of Toogaloo, to Miss Margaret Kemp, both of this District.
Married on the same day, Mr. John Bell of Abbeville District to Miss Ann Elizabeth Watters, of this District.

Issue of April 24, 1807
Died about 11 o'clock A. M. on Wednesday, the 4th ult., at Washington City, the honorable Abraham Baldwin, member of the House of Representatives from Georgia.

Issue of May 8, 1807
On Saturday last Mr. David Craig, a young man about 21 years of age, from Orange County, N. C., in attempting to swim his horse across Keowee River at Gen. Anderson's Ferry, was drowned. On Sunday the body was found and interred.
Died on Wednesday the 29th ult., Mrs. Elizabeth Stribling the amiable consort of Capt. Thomas Stribling, of this District. (eulogy).

Issue of June 5, 1807
Married on Tuesday 26th ult., Mr. Alexander Shaw, of this District, to Miss Susan Harden, daughter of Col. William Harden, of Franklin Co., Ga.

Issue of June 11, 1807
Died on Friday last, Mr. Robert Hammet, a native of England and for a number of year a resident of the village of Pendleton.

Issue of June 25, 1807
Died: at Cambridge, Abbeville District on the 29th ult., Mrs. Elizabeth Montgomery, the amiable and affectionate consort of Rev. Benjamin R. Montgomery.
Died: on Friday last after a long and painful illness, Mrs. Margaret Garvin, wife of Mr. Thomas Garvin Senior, of Pendleton District.

Issue of August 5, 1807
Married on Tuesday, 28th ult., Mr. John Blake Demsey to Miss Elizabeth Rock, both of this District.
Died in Abbeville District, suddenly on the 25th ult., Mr. John McElvany in the 47th year of his age; he had a wife and seven children to lament the loss of an indulgent father and tender husband.

Issue of September 10, 1807
Died on Sunday morning, the 6th inst., Miss Nancy Dickson, youngest daughter of Major Michael Dickson, of this District.

Issue of October 8, 1807
Married on Thursday, the 26th ult., Mr. John Jones of this place to Miss Elizabeth Owens, of Newberry District.

Issue of November 5, 1807
Married This evening by the Rev. Mr. Brown, Samuel Cherry, Esq., merchant of this Village, to Miss Susan Reese, youngest daughter of Mr. Thomas

2

Reese, deceased, of this District.

<u>Issue of November 12, 1807</u>
    Charleston, Nov. 3. Died on Tuesday last, after a painful illness of
45 days, occasioned by a wound he received in a duel, Mr. Samuel Brailsford,
in the 19th year of his age.

<u>Issue of December 3, 1807</u>
    Died on Thursday evening last, of the influenza, John Miller, Sen.
Esquire, in the 63rd year of his age; late Editor of this paper. Those
who were best acquainted with him knew how best to estimate the loss. To
myself irreparable.

<u>Issue of December 10, 1807</u>
    Married on Thursday the 26th ult., by James C. Griffin Esq., Mr. Robert
Brackenridge, English Teacher at the Hopewell Academy, to Miss Elenor
Richards, daughter of Mr. Thomas Richards, of this District.
    Died on Friday the 27th ult., of a Dropsy, Mr. Joseph Jolly Jun., in
the 38th(sic) year of his age, an old and respectable inhabitant of this
District. He has left a widow and seven children to lamentthe loss of an
affectionate husband and parent.

<u>Issue of December 19, 1807</u>
    Married on Tuesday Evening last, Mr. Reuben Hamilton of Pickensville,
to Miss Elizabeth Hallady, of this District.
    Married on Thursday Evening, Mr. Hugh Williams, to Miss Elizabeth Mc-
Guffin, both of this District.

<u>Issue of December 26, 1807</u>
    Died, at Edgefield Court House, on the night of the 4th inst., after
an illness of 24 hours, in the 19th year of her age, Mrs. Joyce Jane Martin,
wife of Charles Martin, Jun. Esq., Attorney at Law.

<u>Issue of January 2, 1808</u>
    Married on Thursday evening by J. C. Griffin, Mr. Alexander Deale, to
Miss Margaret Lawrence, daughter of Mr. Benjamin Lawrence, both of this
District.
    Married on Thursday last, Mr. Benjamin Gasaway to Miss Margaret Hall,
both of this District.

<u>Issue of January 9, 1808</u>
    Married on Tuesday evening by Rev. Mr. Brown, Doctor John Hunter of
this place to Miss Catherine Pickens, youngest daughter of Gen. Andrew
Pickens, of this District.

<u>Issue of January 23, 1808</u>
    Married on Tuesday last by the Rev. Mr. Vandiver, Mr. Aaron Steele to
Miss Elizabeth Massey, both of this District.

<u>Issue of February 13, 1808</u>
    Died suddenly on Friday the 5th inst., Mr. Thomas Harbin, an old and
respectable inhabitant of this District.

<u>Issue of February 20, 1808</u>
    Married on the 11th inst., by Rev. Dr. Waddle, at the Grotto, near
Cambridge, the seat of Mrs. Dunlap, widow of the late John Dunlap, Esq.,
Attorney at Law, the Rev. Mr. Benjamin Ray Montgomery, to that very accomplished and amiable Lady, possessed of an independent estate of Considerable
Value.
    Departed this life on Sunday morning the 7th inst., Mrs. Mary Jones,
the wife of Adam Crain Jones Esq., of Abbeville District, aged 68 years,
a most affectionate wife for 53 years (eulogy).
    Died on Monday the 15th inst., after a long and painful illness which
he bore with Christian fortitude and resignation, in the 68th year of his
age, the Rev. Mr. John Simpson, rector of the Presbyterian Churches on
Generostee (eulogy).
    Died in Abbeville District on the 26th January, Capt. Andrew Bowie, of
the Cavalry, son of Major John Bowie, in the 34th year of his age. He has
left, besides a numerous Circle of friends and relatives, a widow and four
small children to lament his loss.

Issue of February 27, 1808

Married on Sunday evening by Jas. Griffin, Esq., Mr. Thomas Baldwin, to Miss Sally Shenault, both of this District.

Died on the 17th inst., after a long and painful illness, in the 68th year of his age, John Tate, Esq., an old and respectable inhabitant of this District.

Issue of March 5, 1808

Married on the 21st ult., by John McMillion Esq., Mr. John Chapple to Miss Jane Allen, both of this District.

Married on the 28th ult., Mr. Thomas Power, to Miss Zilly Anderson, both of this District.

Married on the 23rd ult., by the Rev. Mr. Moses Holland, Mr. Robert Hemphill to Miss Sibe Sissom, both of this District.

Married on the 23rd ult., by John Tippins, Esq., Mr. William Bennett to Miss Abigail Gee, both of this District.

Issue of March 19, 1808

Married by James Turner Esq., Mr. Daniel Liddell to Miss Isabella Liddell, daughter of Mr. Moses Liddell, deceased, on the 23d ult.

Married on the 18th ult., Mr. Moses Liddell to Miss Sally M'Gee, all of this District.

Married on Thursday the 3rd inst., by John Cochran Esq., Mr. George Brown, son of Col. John Brown, to Miss Jane Barton, daughter of Benjamin Barton, Esq., both of this District.

Issue of March 26, 1808

Baltimore, Feb. 18. Died after a few days illness at Wilmington (Del.) on Sunday morning, John Dickinson, Esq., a character venerable for his years, admired for his talents, respected for his virtues, highly esteemed for his services to his country in the most arduous and difficult times of the revolution.

Issue of April 2, 1808

Married on Tuesday the 8th ult., by B. Starret, Esq., Mr. Andrew Miller to Mrs. Racheal F. Crawford, both of this District.

Issue of April 9, 1808

Married on Thursday last by John Willson Esq., Capt. John Dickson, to Miss Lydia Tourtelot, both of this District.

Issue of April 16, 1808

Married on Thursday last, by Robert M'Cann, Esq., Mr. James M'Kinnie, merchant to Miss Susannah Bates, both of this District.

Issue of June 11, 1808

Married on Sunday Evening, the 5th inst., by John Cleveland, Esq., Dr. Thomas Sherrer to Miss Sarah Brooks, both of this District.

Issue of July 9, 1808

Married on Sunday evening the 26th ult., by John Barton, Esq., Mr. Rolin Patterson, to Miss Nancy Williams; Mr. Dread Williams to Miss Charlotte Honey; Mr. Barnet Morris to Miss Betsey Honey, all of this District.

Married on the 5th inst., by Rev. Mr. Moses Holland, Mr. Howard Ducksworth to Miss Desy Forsythe; on the 16th ult., Mr. William Cox to Miss Francis Gray, all of this District.

Issue of July 30, 1808

Married on the 17th inst., by the Rev. Mr. Vandever, Mr. Andrew Mason to Miss Elizabeth Eaves, both of this District.

Issue of August 6, 1808

Died on Friday last, Master James Melin, about 14 years of age. In attempting to run a horse over the race paths at Pickensville on the 29th ult., the horse broke into the woods and struck his rider against a tree, and fractured his scull.

Issue of August 13, 1808
It is reported and we fear with too much truth, that a duel was fought on Tuesday last, on the Georgia side of the river between James Lesley, an attorney, and Dr. Bochelle, both of Abbeville district; Mr. Lesly was shot through the body and died in a few hours.

Issue of August 20, 1808
Died on the 11th inst., at Andersonville, of apoplexy, Mr. Daniel Costen, a native of Ireland, late of Charleston.

Died on Monday night inst., Miss Jane Carson, aged 16 years; daughter of Mr. James Carson of this District.

Died on Tuesday last, Mrs. Jane Wilson, aged 50; wife of Mr. William Wilson, near Pickensville, in this District.

Issue of August 27, 1808
Married at Rutherfordton, N. C. on Thursday, the 18th inst., Mr. John Eakin, merchant, to Miss Sally Walker, both of that place.

Issue of February 17, 1810
Died on Tuesday last, Mrs. Mitchell, wife of Mr. Joseph Mitchell, of this District.

Issue of February 24, 1810
Married on Thursday last by the Rev. George Brown, Mr. Robert Kelton to the amiable and accomplished Miss Catherine Houston, second daughter of Samuel Houston, Esq., all of this District.

Died on Sunday the 11th inst., Mr. Samuel Bruster the father and on Sunday the 18th inst., Master Henry Bruster, aged 14 years, eldest son of Mr. Samuel Bruster, deceased, of this District.

Issue of March 10, 1810
Married on Thursday last, by John Simpson, Esq., Mr. Robert Allen of the Indiana Territory to Miss Margaret Dodds, of this District.

Issue of March 24, 1810
Married on Thursday last, by the Rev. George Vandever, Mr. Abraham J. Hargiss, to Miss Elizabeth Kilpatrick, both of this District.

Died on Sunday the 18th inst., Mr. John Ramsay, son of Mr. Alexander Ramsay, and student of Physic near this place (eulogy).

Died yesterday, Mr. David Wadkins, long a respectable inhabitant of this District.

Issue of March 31, 1810
Married on Thursday the 15th inst., by Obediah Trimmier, Esq., Capt. Thomas Stribling, to Miss Catherine Hamilton, daughter of Adjutant James Hamilton, decd., all of this District.

Married on Tuesday the 20th inst., Capt. Cain Broyles of this District, to Miss Lucinda Nash, of Abbeville District.

Married on Thursday last, by John Cochran, Esq., Mr. Isaac Melson to Miss Nancy Morrow, both of this District.

Died on Saturday evening last, Mr. Henry Bruster, son of Mr. James Bruster, deceased; he has left a widow and two young children to deplore their irreparable loss.

Issue of April 7, 1810
Died on Friday the 9th ult., at his residence in Darlington District, the Hon. Samuel Wilds, one of the Judges of the Court of Common Pleas and Sessions of this state, within a few hours of the day which would have completed his 35th year.

Issue of April 14, 1810
Married on Thursday last by John Willson, Esq., Mr. Hugh M'Kinney to Miss Elizabeth Smith, daughter of Mr. Benjamin Smith.

Married on Thursday evening by the Rev. James Hembree, Mr. George Kennedy to Miss Fanny Jolly, daughter of Mr. James Jolly, all of this District.

Died on Friday last, Mrs. Sarah Ward, aged 80 years.

Issue of April 21, 1810
    Married on Tuesday the 17th inst., James Osborn, Esq., merchant of Pickensville, to the amiable Miss Patsey Terrel, both of this District.

Issue of June 23, 1810
    Died on Thursday the 14th inst., Mrs. Grissom, wife of John Grissom, Esq. of this District.

Issue of July 28, 1810
    Married on Thursday the 19th inst. by the Rev. James Hembree, Mr. Benj. Winn to Miss Sarah Patterson.
    Married on the same day, Mr. Aaron Smith to Miss Smith, daughter of Mr. Nimrod Smith, all of this District.

Issue of August 4, 1810
    Drowned on Saturday the 28th ult., Mr. Carey Brown, aged 20 years, 2 months and 18 days; a son of Mr. George Brown, a reputable citizen of this District.
    On Wednesday the 25th ult., Master William De La Fletcher Keys, son of Peter Keys, Esq., aged seven years and eight months., received a kick from a horse on the head, which he survived about 14 hours.
    Died on the night of Wednesday the 1st inst., Mrs. Mary M. Dart, the amiable and lamented wife of Mr. Thomas L. Dart, near this place.

Issue of September 1, 1810
    Married on Tuesday evening last, by the Rev. Mr. Price of James Island, the Rev. John D. Murphy, late of Robeson County, N. C. to Miss Jane M. McElhenny, daughter of Rev. James McElhenny of Pendleton District.

Issue of September 8, 1810
    Died on Saturday the 25th ult., Mrs. Elenor McDaniel, wife of Mr. James McDaniel, of this District.

Issue of October 8, 1810
    Columbia, Sept. 22. Departed this life at his residence near this place, Mr. Samuel Cobb, late of Pendleton District, leaving an afflicted widow and bereaved children.

Issue of November 3, 1810
    Died on the 26th ult., Master William Walker, aged 8 years and 22 days, son of Mr. William Walker, on Eighteen Mile Creek in this District.
    Departed this transitory life, on the 23d ult., in the 45th year of her age, Mrs. Letitia Keys, wife of Peter Keys, Esq., of this District. She embraced religion in her early days under the Methodist ministry.

Issue of November 24, 1810
    Died on Tuesday the 20th inst., in the 17th year of his age, the picture of rosy health, Mr. John Gates, son of Mr. Charles Gates, of this District.
    Died on Thursday the 22nd inst., Mr. James Gilkison, a native of Ireland, but for a considerable time a respectable inhabitant of this District.

Issue of December 22, 1810
    Married on the 6th inst., by Richard Holden, Esq., Capt. A. Roe, to the amiable Miss Patsey Birch, daughter of Henry Birch, Esq., both of this District.
    Died in Spartanburgh in October last, at her son's plantation, in the 42nd year of her age, Mrs. Rebeca Laval, of Charleston, wife of Major Laval, of the United States Army.

Issue of December 29, 1810
    Died, at Columbia, on Thursday evening, the 20th inst., Michael Hammond, Esq. of this place.

Issue of January 19, 1811
Married on Thursday the 10th inst., by Samuel Dickson, Esq., Mr. Daniel Camp to Miss Ann Cason, both of this District.

Issue of July 17, 1813
Married on Tuesday the 6th inst., by the Rev. Robert Orr, Mr. James Orr to Miss Ann Anderson,daughter of Capt. James Anderson Senior, of this District.
Married on Thursday the 8th inst., by the Rev. Barr, Mr. Joseph Grisham of this place, to Miss Ann Watt, daughter of Samuel Watt, Esq., decd. of Abbeville District.

Issue of July 24, 1813
Died on Sunday Evening, last near this place, Mr. William Gourley, aged 21 years.

Issue of July 31, 1813
Married on Thursday the 15th inst., by the Rev. Geo. Brown, Mr. William Elrod to Miss Rosanna M'Kay, all of this district.

Issue of August 14, 1813
Married on Thursday last, by C. Gaillard, Esq., Mr. Wm. Rodgers to Miss Mary Ann Moore, all of this district.

Issue of August 21, 1813
Married on Thursday last by the Rev. George Vandivere, Mr. Wm. Ward of Lawrence, to Miss Sarah Reeder, daughter of Mr. Jonathan Reeder, of this District.
Married on Friday the 13th inst., by the Rev. Wm. Barr, Mr. Alexander Spears, student of Law of Abbeville District, to the amiable and accomplished Miss Eliza Middleton, daughter of Major Hugh Middleton, decd., of Edgefield District.

Issue of September 11, 1813
Died, on the 8th inst., at his plantation in this district, Capt. James Anderson Senior, much lamented by his relatives.

Issue of September 25, 1813
Married on Thursday the 9th inst., by George Manning, Esq., Mr. Thomas Stevenson to Miss Elizabeth Collins.
Married on Tuesday last, by A. Liddell, Esq., Mr. David Rosier to Miss Nelly Carter, all of this district.

Issue of October 16, 1813
Married on Friday the 24th ult., by Charles Gaillard, Esq., Mr. Aaron Philips, to Miss Ruth Perkins, daughter of Capt. Wm. Perkins.
Married on Thursday the 7th inst., by A. Liddell, Esq., Mr. Charles Richie, to Miss Polly Heaton, all of this District.

Issue of October 30, 1813
Married on Thursday the 14th inst., by A. Liddell, Esq., Mr. Reuben Anderson, to Miss Sucky Welsh.
Married on Thursday the 21st inst. by James C. Griffin, Esq., Mr. Aaron Mullinax to Mrs. Rebecca Voyles, all of this district.
Melancholy Accident. On Sunday the 17th inst., Mr. Benjamin Harrison, the son and four young girls, the daughters of Mr. Thomas Harrison, together with two young negro fellows, one belonging to Mr. Lewis Ralston, the other to Mr. Chearham of Georgia. three girls aged 14, 11 and 9 drowned and one negro.

Issue of November 13, 1813
Married on Tuesday last, by Samuel Houston, Esq., Mr. William Kilpatrick to the amiable Miss Elizabeth Gray, eldest daughter of John Gray, Esq.
Married on the same evening, by S. Houston, Esq., Mr. _____ Robinson of Haywood, N. C. to Miss Polly Robinson of this district.
Died on Thursday the 21st ult., at Mr. William Gatton's, after a short illness, Mr. Michael Warnock, of this district.

Issue of November 27, 1813
Charleston, Nov. 13. Died on the 9th inst., at his residence in George

Street, Peter Freneau, Esq., aged 57 years.
Married on Thursday the 2nd inst., by the Rev. A. Brown, Mr. Wm. M'-
Clure to Miss Elizabeth White, both of this district.

Issue of December 25, 1813
Died on the 10th inst., after a short but painful illness, Miss Isabella Liddell, daughter of Mr. Andrew J. Liddell, aged 8 years, three months
and 13 days.

Issue of February 5, 1814
Married on the 20th ult., by the Rev. Wm. H. Barr, Alex Bowie, Esq., to
Miss Susan B. Jack, all of Abbeville District.

Issue of April 8, 1818
Melancholy Accident. On Wed. evening last, Mrs. Stonecypher and her
infant, Miss Jane Sims, and a young lad her brother, were crossing Toga-
loo River at a ford at Mr. Cleveland's, but not being acquainted with the
plce, got into deep water and were carried down the river. Mrs. Stonecypher
the child, and Miss Sims were drowned, the boy swam ashore, and also both
the horses were saved. The body of the infant has been found, of the
others, no discovery has yet been made.

Issue of May 6, 1818
Married on Tuesday the 21st ult., by Rev. Lewis Rector, Mr. William E.
Blassingame, to Miss Eliza Towns, only daughter of Wm. Towns Esq., all of
Greenville district.

Issue of June 17, 1818
Married on Thursday evening last, by James C. Griffen, Esq., Mr. John
Hays to Miss Sarah Howell, second daughter of Mr. Abner Howell, all of
this district.
Died on the 2nd inst., Mr. John Lewis an old inhabitant of this place
-- he has left a large family deeply impressed with the loss....
Died on Friday last, after a short illness, Miss Rebecca Garret, aged
18 years.

Issue of July 8, 1818
On Saturday last, Mr. Isaac Williams who lived near this place, being
out deer hunting, received the bite of a rattlesnake, and died.

Issue of July 15, 1818
Married on the 7th inst., by the Rev. James Hillhouse, Mr. David Moseley, to Miss Eliza Barton, daughter of Mr. Benjamin Barton, decd., all
of this district.

Issue of August 12, 1818
On the 27th ult., Mr. John Stuart, a citizen of this district was shot;
while working in his gunsmith's shop; he died a short time afterwards.

Issue of August 26, 1818
Married on the 13th inst., by the Rev. James Hillhouse, Mr. Joseph
Pitts of Newberry, to Miss Ann Lemon, daughter of Mr. Robert Lemon, of
this District.
Died on Friday last, Mrs. Mary Warnock, of a Hydrothorax, aged 85
years...one of the first settlers in this district.
Died on Monday last, Mr. Hartwell Hunnicutt, of a Hydrothorax, aged
90 years; an honest, respectable, and one of the first inhabitants of this
district. He was a soldier at Braddock's defeat, and a regular soldier
in the service of the United States' during the Revolutionary War.
Died on Sunday last, aged 17 years, Mrs. Elizabeth Terrell, wife of
Henry Terrell, Esq., of this district...She died on the day she attained
her 17th year, the same hour of the day, and the same room in the house
where she was born.

Issue of September 9, 1818
Married on Thursday last, by the Rev. Lewis Rector, Doctor John Robert-
son, to Miss Eliza Blassingame, daughter of Gen. John Blassingame, all of
G'ville district.

8

Issue of September 16, 1818
Died on the 13th inst., at this place, of an abscess on the liver, Lieut. Wm. Edmondson, late of the U. S. army, aged 32 years, a son of Wm. Edmondson, Esq., of Pickensville.
Died on the same day, Alfred White, aged 3 years and 9 months, son of Mr. Asa White of this place.

Issue of September 23, 1818
Died on the 19th inst., of a nervous fever in the 14th year of her age, Miss Isabella McGuffin, youngest daughter of Mr. Wm. McGuffin of this district.

Issue of September 30, 1818
Married on Thursday the 24th inst., by Rev. Andrew Brown, Mr. Arthur Craig to Miss Lucinda Grisham, daughter of John Grisham, Esq., all of this District.
Died on the 28th inst., after a long illness, which she bore with fortitude and resignation, Mrs. Elizabeth Maverick, aged 35 years, wife of Mr. Samuel Maverick.

Issue of October 7, 1818
Married on Thursday the ___ ult., by James C. Griffen, Esq., Mr. Henry McCrary, to Miss Catherine Dickson, daughter of Benjamin Dickson, Esq., all of this District.

Issue of October 14, 1818
Died on the 12th inst., Mr. Christopher Kirksey, Sen. aged 84 years; an old and respectable inhabitant of this district.
Died on Saturday last, Mr. James Ramey, aged 23 years.

Issue of October 21, 1818
Died on Wednesday the 7th inst., of the milk sickness, Miss Mary Crosby, aged 32 years.
Died on Sunday last, Mr. Lloyd Mullinax, in the 20th year of his age.

Issue of October 28, 1818
Married on Wednesday last, by the Rev. James Hillhouse, Mr. Alexander Morrow to Miss Mary Morrow; both of this district.
Married on Thursday last, by the Rev. James Hillhouse, Mr. John Miller Junior, of this place, to Miss Lydia Ann Perdreau, of St. James, Santee.

Issue of January 6, 1819
Married on the 15th of December last, at the Black Warrior, Lieut. Col. Hugh Harrison, of the 18th Reg. S. C. militia to Miss Judith Kilpatrick, late of this District.
Married on the 24th ult., by the Rev. Mr. Quarles, Mr. Lemuel Brown, of Cane Creek, to Mrs. Sarah Shannon, on Conneros.

Issue of February 3, 1819
Married on the 17th ult., by Abner Steele, Esq., Mr. John Wright to Miss Fanny Sherley, both of Choestoe.
Married on the 10th ult., by John Verner, Esq., Mr. Flowry Swift, of Franklin County, Ga., to Miss Sarah Fitzgerald, of this District.
Married on the 21st ult., by the Rev. Mr. Calloway, Mr. Clement Thompson of Abbeville, to Miss Elizabeth Davies of Choestoe.
Married on Monday the 25th ult., at Asheville, N. C. by the Rev. Francis H. Porter, Mr. John Hall, merchant of Pendleton, S. C. to Miss Caroline Swain of that place.

Issue of March 3, 1819
Married on Thursday last, by the Rev. James Hillhouse, Mr. Wm. McCay to Miss Mary White, both of this District.

Issue of March 10, 1819
James Meek Senior of York District was drowned on Wednesday the 3d inst., while attempting to cross Seneca River, at Col. Anderson's ferry. ...on his way to attend the ensuing land sales in Alabama, and had mistaken directions.

Issue of March 17, 1819
Married on the 9th inst., by the Rev. James Hillhouse, Mr. James
Davis to Miss Jane Lemon,daughter of Mr. Robert Lemon, all of this District.

Issue of April 21, 1819
Married on Thursday last, by the Rev. James Hillhouse, Mr. Wm. Boggs
to Miss Letitia Hamilton, daughter of Mr. Thomas Hamilton, all of this
District.

Issue of April 28, 1819
Married on Thursday last,by James Cooper, Esq., Mr. James Hobson Sen.
aged 71 years, to Miss Polly Wilson aged 20 years, all of this District.

Issue of May 12, 1819
Married on Thursday last, by the Rev. James Hillhouse, Mr. David K.
Hamilton, to Miss Jane Walker, daughter of Mr. William Walker, all of
this District.

Issue of February 9, 1820
Married on Tuesday evening the 1st inst., by the Rev. Mr. Gibson,
Mr. Micajah Webb, of Pendleton District, to Miss Harriet Benson, daugh-
ter of Major Thomas Benson of Greenville District.
Married on Thursday night last, by John Lee, Esq., Mr. Joseph Sisk
to Miss Nancy Hubbard, daughter of Mr. Luke Hubbard.
Married on Thursday the 6th ult., by the Rev. Mr. Portwood, Mr. Wm.
Crosby, aged 81 years to Mrs. Ann Fortner, all of this district.

Issue of February 16, 1820
Married on Thursday last by Andrew J. Liddell, Esq., Mr. Joshua
Rainwater, to Miss Polly Peterson, all of this district.
Died on Saturday the 5th inst., Mr. Andrew Robinson of this dis-
trict, by a fall from his horse on returning from muster.

Issue of April 5, 1820
Married on the 27th ult., by the Rev. James Hillhouse, Mr. Lawrence
Sims to Miss Renny Harris, both of this district.
Died on the 30th ult., at the house of Henry M'Cray, Esq., on Choes-
toe, in this district, in the 77th year of her age, Mrs. Nancy Watson,
late of Rutherford County, N. C.

Issue of April 12, 1820
Died on Friday, the 17th inst., Mr. Hollingsworth Vendevere Sen., of
a long and lingering illness, aged 90 years. He was born in the State of
Maryland, but for the last 28 years, a respectable citizen of this district.

Issue of May 3, 1820
Died on the 25th ult., Mr. Nathaniel Davis, aged 73 years, an old
inhabitant of this district.
Died on the 29th ult., Mrs. Elizabeth Prater, aged 39 years, wife of
Mr. John Prater of this district.

Issue of May 17, 1820
Married on the 15th inst., by Joseph Grisham, Esq., Mr. John Welch
to Miss Elizabeth Hubbard, daughter of Luke Hubbard, all of this
district.
Died on the 8th inst., Mrs. Thomas Carradine, aged 70 years, an old
inhabitant of this district.

Issue of May 24, 1820
Died on the night of Saturday last, after a long and painful illness
in the 45th year of her age, Mrs. Anne Miller, wife of Mr. Crosby W.
Miller of this place...left an affectionate husband and ten children....

Issue of June 14, 1820
Married on Tuesday the 6th inst., by Joseph Grisham, Esq., Mr. William
Hunnicut to Miss Catherine P. M'Guffen, all of this district.
Married on Thursday last by William Carson, Esq., Mr. Abner Crosby
to Miss Edith Smith, all of this district.

It is stated in the Columbia paper, received at Greenville, that the death of Rev. Doctor Maxcy, Pres. of the S. C. College, occurred on Sunday the 4th inst. We have not heard the particulars.

Issue of June 21, 1820
    Married on the 15th inst., by Joseph Grisham, Esq. James C. Griffen, Esq. to Mrs. Sophia Doyle, all of this district.
    Died on the 9th inst., Miss Jane Steele, an inhabitant of this district...(eulogy).

Issue of July 5, 1820
    Married on the 16th inst., by Wm. Carson, Esq., Mr. James W. Drennan to Miss Elizabeth Beck, all of this district.

Issue of August 2, 1820
    Died on the 15th ult., Capt. William Lynch, aged 78 years. He was an old revolutionary soldier...and a good farmer...(eulogy).

Issue of August 9, 1820
    Died on the 6th ult., after a long and painful illnes, Mr. Robert Dowdle, aged 76 years, and for the last 36, a resident of this district. He was a member of the Presbyterian Church...left a widow and several children...(eulogy).

Issue of August 16,1820
    Died on the 10th ult., near Fort Jackson, his Excellency William Bibb, Governor of the State of Alabama.

Issue of September 27, 1820
    Married on the 4th inst., by Wm. Carson, Esq., Mr. Levi Phillips to Miss Rachel Johnson.
    Married on the 14th inst., Mr. Sidney Robertson, to Miss Nancy Hull, all of this district.

Issue of October 4, 1820
    Married on the 7th ult., by Green Smith, Esq., Capt. William Verner of this district to Miss Eleanor Hooper, daughter of Matthew Hooper, Esq., of Franklin County, Georgia.

Issue of October 11, 1820
    Married on the 3rd inst., by the Rev. Robert Gaines, Mr. George Gillespie to Miss Ann Cooper, eldest daughter of James Cooper, Esq., of this place.
    Married on the 3rd inst. by W. M. Carson, Esq., Capt. Alexander Latta, to Miss Elenor Birtchfield, all of this district.
    An inquest was held on the 7th inst., by Joseph Grisham, Esq., coroner, on the body of Mrs. Elizabeth Martin, wife of Mr. Samuel Martin of this district. The jury returned the verdict that she was murdered.

Issue of October 25, 1820
    Married on the 19th inst., by Nathan Boon, Esq., Mr. Wm. Hall to Miss Sebrey Peterson, daughter of Mr. John Peterson, all of this district.
    Married on the 19th inst., by John Verner, Esq., Mr. John Anderson to Miss Mary Clanahan, daughter of Mr. Robert Clanahan, all of this district.

Issue of November 8, 1820
    Married on Thursday the 2nd inst., in Greenville District, by the Rev. James Hillhouse, Dr. Samuel Earle of this place, to Miss Harriet Wright, of Greenville District.

Issue of November 15, 1820
    Died on the 7th inst., aged 62 years, Mr. William Forbes, an old and faithful soldier during the revolutionary war, and one among the first settlers in the district.

Issue of November 22, 1820
　　Married on Thursday last, by the Rev. James Hillhouse, Joseph V.
Shanklin, Esq., of this place to Miss Ann Lewis, daughter of Col.
Richard Lewis of this district.

Issue of December 13, 1820
　　Married on Thursday the 30th ult., Mr. Wm. Langston to Miss Elizabeth, daughter of Mr. M'Murray, Esq., of this district.

Issue of December 27, 1820
　　Married on Thursday last, by the Rev. James Hillhouse, Capt. John P.
Benson, of this place, to Miss Catherine Sloan, youngest daughter of
Capt. David Sloan, Senior, of this district.
　　Married on Tuesday the 19th inst., by the same, Mr. Reuben Cason to
Miss Jemima Oliver.
　　Married on the 24th inst., at this place by Joseph Grisham, Esq., Mr.
John Raimey to Miss Elizabeth Waldrup.
　　Married on the 26th inst., by the Rev. Robert Gaines, Mr. Willis
Robinson, to Miss Lucy Gassaway, all of this district.
　　Died at the house of Mr. James Hunter, in this district, on the 14th
inst., Mr. Richard Christie, aged 32 years, a native of Ireland.

Issue of January 17, 1821
　　Married on the 4th inst., by Wm. Carson, Esq., Mr. Ephraim Lee, to
Miss Mary, eldest daughter of Mr. John Beck.
　　Married on the 9th inst., by the same, Mr. Thornton Syms, to Miss
Elizabeth, 2d daughter of Aaron Butler, all of this district.

Issue of January 24, 1821
　　Died on Tuesday the 9th inst., Mr. William Cunningham, aged 93
years, an Irishman by birth...came to this country with General Braddock, served as a soldier in the American Army in the Revolution...for
the last 30 years, a resident of this district.

Issue of February 14, 1821
　　Died on Friday last, at Bachelor's Retreat, in this district, in
the 24th year of his age, Mr. William Lee, late of Charleston.

Issue of February 21, 1821
　　Married on Thursday last, by the Rev. James Hillhouse, Mr. Robert
Henderson, to Miss Mary Ann, daughter of Mr. James M'Carley, all of
this district.

Issue of February 28, 1821
　　Married on Friday the 16th inst., by Joseph Grisham, Esq., Mr. Thos.
Williams to Miss Jane Moore.
　　Married by the same on Tuesday the 20th inst., Mr. Willis Prince
to Miss Elizabeth Wimpey, daughter of Mr. Archibald Wimpey, all of
this district.

Issue of March 21, 1821
　　Married on Thursday last, by the Rev. James Hillhouse, Mr. Crosby
Wilkes Miller, to Miss Elizabeth, daughter of Mr. Thomas Hamilton, all
of this District.

Issue of May 2, 1821
　　Died on Monday last at the residence of Mr. John Miller, senior,
near this place, Mr. Stephen Kinsley, of Charleston, aged 34 years, a
native of Ireland. ...a good soldier in the U. S. service, in the last
war.

Issue of May 30, 1821
　　Married on Thursday last, by the Rev. Mr. Dickerson, Mr. Thomas
Lynch Dart, to Miss Mary, third daughter of Mr. Benjamin Dupre, all of
this district.

Issue of June 20, 1821
　　Married on Thursday last, by Joseph Grisham, Esq., Mr. John Brownlow to Miss Susan, daughter of Mr. Elisha Alexander, of this district.

Issue of July 4, 1821
Died suddenly of Apoplexy, on the 12th ult., Mr. Andrew Roe, aged
60 years...an old Revolutionary soldier, and one of the oldest inhabitants of this district.

Issue of July 11, 1821
Married on Thursday the 5th inst., by the Rev. Robert Gaines, Mr.
Frederick Garvin, aged 17 years and nine months to Miss Elizabeth
Clayton, aged 17 years and 5 months,daughter of Mr. William Clayton,all
of this district.

Issue of August 1, 1821
Died on Saturday the 21st ult., at his plantation about five miles
from this place, William Steele, Esq., in the 58th year of his age...one
of the first settlers in this town, where he resided 33 years...left a
wife, four sons, two daughters....

Issue of August 8, 1821
Married on Thursday last, by Joseph Grisham, Esq., Mr. Benjamin
Hopkins, to Miss Margaret, daughter of Mr. John Eaton, all of this
District.

Issue of August 15, 1821
Died on Monday the 13th in child bed, Mrs. Honey, aged 28 years,
wife of Mr. William Honey, of this district.
Died on Thursday the 12th ult., Col. John Taylor, late of this
place. He died at his plantation on the Alabama, 8 or 10 miles below
Cahawba.

Issue of August 22, 1821
Married on Tuesday the 14th inst., by R. Holden, Esq., Mr. Joseph
Morgan to Miss Polly Bryan.
Married on Thursday the 16th inst., by Rev. Robert Gaines, Mr. James
Evett to Miss Rebecca Thompson, daughter of Mr. Wm. Thompson, all of
this District.

Issue of September 12, 1821
Died on Friday the 7th inst., Mrs. Mary Hunnicutt, aged 85 years,
relict of Mr. Hartwell Hunnicutt, late of this District.

Issue of September 19, 1821
Married on Thursday last by the Rev. Mr. Stevens, Mr. David H.
Hopkins, of this place, to Miss Elizabeth, daughter of Mr. Edward
Epps, all of this District.

Issue of September 26, 1821
Married on Sunday the 15th inst., by William Barton, Esq., Mr. William
Pearce to Miss Elizabeth Wooten, all of this District.

Issue of October 3, 1821
Married in Greenville District by Rev. N. Berry, the Rev. Solomon G.
Ward to Mrs. Elizabeth Thermon, of that district.

Issue of October 31, 1821
Died on Monday the 15th inst., Mrs. Millie Lamar, wife of Mr. Nathan
Lamar, all of this district.

Issue of November 28, 1821
Married on Thursday the 22d inst., by Wm. Carson, Esq., Mr. Joseph
Robinson, to Miss Elizabeth, daughter of Mr. Elisha Miller, all of this
District.
Died at Greenville C. H. on Thursday the 8th inst., in the 48th year
of his age, George Washington Earle, Esq., Clerk of Court and Post-Master.
He has left a wife and seven children.

Issue of December 5, 1821
Died on Friday night the 30th ult., of the measles, in the 30th year
of her age, Mrs. Nancy Grisham, wife of Col. Joseph Grisham of this place.
A husband and three children survive her (eulogy).

Died in Edgefield District, on the 15th ult., aged 67 years, Major General William Butler, of the 1st Division of the Militia of S. C.

Issue of December 12, 1821
Died yesterday morning, in the 56th year of his age, Mr. Rolin Hunnicutt. He was an old inhabitant of this district. A good neighbor and an honest inoffensive citizen.

Issue of December 19, 1821
Married on Thursday last, by the Rev. James Hembree, Mr. Jesse Cobb to Miss Lucy second daughter of James C. Griffin, Esq., all of this district.

Issue of January 2, 1822
Married on Thursday last, by the Rev. James Hillhouse, Capt. Daniel Towers, to Miss Margaret Brown, daughter of Mr. Alexander Brown, all of this district.

Issue of January 9, 1822
Married on Tuesday the 1st inst., by the Rev. James Hillhouse, Robert Maxwell, Esq., to Miss Mary, daughter of Samuel Earle, Esq., all of this district.

Issue of January 23, 1822
Died on Wednesday the 9th inst., at this place, Miss Elizabeth Evans, aged 16.

Issue of February 27, 1822
Married last evening by Jos. Grisham, Esq., Mr. Andrew Van Dyke, to Miss Sarah Hubbard, all of this district.

Issue of March 6, 1822
Married in Charleston, on the 21st ult., by the Rev. Rodolphus Dickinson, Col. John Ewing Calhoun, of this District to Miss Martha Maria, youngest daughter of Capt. William Ransom Davis, decd, formerly of High Hills of Santee.

Issue of March 20, 1822
Died near Jefferson, in the state of Georgia, on Tuesday the 12th inst. Mrs. Anna Orr, wife of Mr. James Orr, formerly of this District....left a husband and four children.
Melancholy Accident. Four of five children of Mr. and Mrs. Nathan Mason perished in a fire.

Issue of March 27, 1822
Married on Thursday the 14th inst., by Wm. Carson, Esq., Mr. John Robinson to Miss Patsey Barie.
Married on Tuesday the 19th inst., by the same, Mr. Mathew McDaniel to Miss Susannah McGuffin, all of this District.

Issue of April 17, 1822
Married on Monday the 8th inst. by the Rev. James Hillhouse, Doctor James Oliver, to Miss M. Leeh, all of this District.
Died on Monday the 8th inst, of the measles, Mr. John Mullinax, aged 27.

Issue of May 1, 1822
Died at his residence near this place on the 25th inst., Doctor William Hunter, in the 47th year of his age...left a widow and nine children....

Issue of May 22, 1822
Died on Friday evening last, after a short illness, Miss Nancy Duff, daughter of Capt. James Duff, decd. (eulogy).
Died on Sunday evening last, Mrs. Margaret C. Taliaferro, aged 54 years, wife of Zechariah Taliaferro, Esq....left a husband and four daughters.

Issue of June 19, 1822
Married on Thursday last, by Robert McCann, Esq., Mr. Sidney Forbes of Alabama, to Miss Laura Robinson, daughter of Mr. Ephraim Robinson, of this District.

14

Issue of July 31, 1822
Married on Thursday the 18th inst., by Rev. Mr. S. Vandevere, Mr. Richard B. Robinson to Miss Polly Bruster, daughter of Mr. Samuel Bruster, all of this district.

Issue of August 14, 1822
Married on Tuesday the 6th inst., by William Carson, Esq., Mr. Sidney Cole to Miss Sarah Jones.
Married on the same day by the same, Mr. Major Cole to Miss Fanny Jones, all of this district.

Issue of August 21, 1822
Died on the 12th inst., Mrs. Euphemia Johnston, wife of Mr. Richard Johnston, of this district...left a husband and seven small children....

Issue of September 11, 1822
Died on Thursday last, in the 81st year of her age, Mrs. Mary Story, a native of Pennsylvania, and for many years an inhabitant of this district.
Married on Thursday the 29th ultimo, by the Rev. David Qualls, Mr. Lewis Frick to Miss Elizabeth Vice, both of this District.

Issue of October 2, 1822
Married on Thursday the 26th ultimo, by the Rev. Barnet Smith, the Rev. James Dannelly to Miss Keziah Linn, daughter of James Linn, Esq., of this District.
Married on Thursday the 13th ult., by the Rev. Sandford Vandivere, Mr. Moses Dean, to Miss Narcissa Lewis, daughter of Major Lewis, all of this District.
Married on Tuesday last, by the Rev. James Hillhouse, Mr. Benjamin Sloan, to Miss Eliza, daughter of Gen. John B. Earle of this district.

Issue of October 16, 1822
Married on Thursday last at Westville, the residence of Col. Robert Anderson, by the Rev. James Hillhouse, Mr. Ezekiel Harris to Miss Jane Y. Thomas, all of this district.

Issue of October 30, 1822
Married on Thursday last, by the Rev. Mr. Stevens, Mr. Elijah Coffee to Miss Nancy, daughter of Mr. Hardy Owens, all of this district.
Married on Thursday by Robert White, Esq., Mr. Curtis to Miss Sarah Boon, daughter of William Boon, Esq., of this district.

Issue of December 4, 1822
Married last evening by the Rev. James Douthit, Col. Joseph Grisham, of this village, to Miss Mary, eldest daughter of Mr. William Steele, Esq., deceased, late of this district.
Truly melancholy. On the 12th of November last, Mr. William Cape, living in this district was crossing the Creek on a log with three children, two of his own and Elizabeth Ann King,; they all fell off, and two of the children were drowned. The body of the boy has been found, but they were still looking for the girl when our informant left there.

Issue of December 11, 1822
Married yesterday evening, by the Rev. Rodolphus Dickinson, Mr. James O. Lewis to Miss Mary T., eldest daughter of Mr. Thomas Lorton, of this place.

Issue of December 18, 1822
Married on Tuesday the 3d inst., by Rev. Isaiah Stephens, Mr. Elijah Gillison, to Miss Mary Ann, eldest daughter of Capt. John Abbot, all of this district.

Issue of December 25, 1822
Died on the 2d inst., at the residence of her son, Jesse Stribling, Esq., Mrs. Ann Stribling, aged 91 years.

Issue of January 8, 1823
Married on the 23d ult., by Henery Terrel, Esq., Mr. Stephen C. Reed, to Miss Sarah Barton, all of this district.

Issue of January 15, 1823
Died on the 10th inst., John Willson, Esq., aged 83 years, an old soldier of the Revolution, and served under Gen. Pickens most of the war. For a number of year he was Senator in the State Legislature from this District, and at different times has held offices of public trust...an Elder of the Presbyterian Church at Carmel; a kind parent and neighbor....

Issue of January 29, 1823
Married on Thursday last, by James C. Griffin, Esq., Mr. Joseph Pinson, of this place to Miss Mary Mills, daughter of Mr. Hugh Mills, of this district.

Issue of February 5, 1823
Departed this life on the 30th ult., in the 38th year of her age, Mrs. Mary Elizabeth Gaillard, consort of Mr. Josias D. Gaillard (eulogy).
From the Charleston Courier: We record with deep concern the death of our distinguished fellow-citizen, the Hon. William Lowndes, who died on board the ship Moss at sea, on 27th Oct. on his way to Europe for the recovery of his health.

Issue of February 12, 1823
Married on Thursday the 30th ult., by the Rev. Richard Gaines, Mr. Thomas B. Reid to Miss Sarah Nicholson, daughter of William Nicholson, Esq., deceased; all of this district.

Issue of February 19, 1823
Died on Monday last, Mr. John Creaton, aged 32 years, a native of Ireland, a citizen of this district about two years....left a wife and four children.
Married on Tuesday the 11th inst., by Wm. Carson, Esq., Mr. John Lee to Miss Isabella, fourth daughter of Mr. John Beck, all of this district.

Issue of February 26, 1823
Married on Tuesday the 18th inst., by Rev. Anthony Ross, Mr. Felix Watkins to Miss Elenor Robinson, both of this district.

Issue of March 5, 1823
Died on Tuesday night, the 25th ult., Mrs. Milly Cain, wife of Mr. John Cain of this district...about 35 years of age, and left her husband and seven children.

Issue of March 26, 1823
Married on Thursday last, by the Rev. Rodolphus Dickinson, Doctor Ozey R. Broyles to Miss Sarah Ann Taliaferro, eldest daughter of Zacharias Taliaferro, Esq., all of this district.

Issue of April 16, 1823
Died on Monday the 7th inst., Mr. John Sanders of this district. His death was occasioned by a fall from his horse.

Issue of May 21, 1823
Married on Thursday the 8th inst., by the Rev. Joseph Hillhouse, Doctor William Calhoun Norris, of Pendleton, to Miss Elvira Thompson, only daughter of John Thompson, Esq., of Union District.
Married on Sunday night, the 11th inst., by Robert McCann, Esq., Mr. Alfred Moore, to Miss Darcus King, all of this district.
Married in Fairfield District, Mr. Reuben Pickett to Miss Rebecca Lewis, daughter of William Lewis, Esq.
Died in Alabama, John W. Walker, Esq., late of Senator of the U. S.
Died at Mobile, the 20th ult., Taliaferro Livingston, Esq., U. S. Marshal of the district of Alabama, aged 41.
Died at Lumberton, N. C., on the 16th ult., Richard Shackelford, late sheriff of Georgetown District, aged 42.
Died on Waccamaw on the 23d ult., in the 22d year of her age, Mrs. Elizabeth Rowell, wife of Mr. B. W. Rowell.

Issue of May 28, 1823
Married, Mr. John Martin Miller of Columbia, to Miss Margaret M.
Bird, of Edgefield district (date not given).
Married at Clear Spring, Colonel H. B. Armstrong, of New-York, to
Miss Mary D. Simons, daughter of Major James Simons, deceased.
Married: Mr. James Dearly to Miss Jane Green, daughter of Mr. Samuel
Green, of black River.   Capt. James Carson to Miss Susan Tarbox, of
Georgetown. Lately in England, Mrs. Patterson, of Baltimore, Maryland,
formerly Madame Jerome Bonaparte, to the young Earl of Cholmondely and
Lady Harvey, formerly Miss Caton, also of Baltimore, and relict of Col.
Harvey, aid-de-camp to the Duke of Wellington, to Lord Petre, nephew to
the Duke of Norfolk.
Married at Westerlo, N. Y. on the 1st inst., by Rev. Berrian
Hotchkins, Deacon, Daniel Jewel, of Greenville, in the 82d year to Mrs.
Mary Allen, Grandmother to the late lamented Lieut. Allen, in her 85th
year. She being his fourth wife. The above worthy and extraordinary
couple have been many year respectable members of the Presbyterian Church
in Greenville.
Died in Winsborough (sic), S. C., Mrs. Margaret Moore, consort of
Major Mm. (sic) Moore.
Died on the 25th ult., in Union district, Mr. Garret Hendricks, aged
107 years.

Issue of June 4, 1823
Married on the 20th ult., by the Rev. Wm. B. Johnston, Mr. Thomas
Jones, of Laurens, to Miss Emily Thompson, daughter of the Hon. W.
Thompson, of Greenville, S. C.
Married on Tuesday 30th ult., by the Rev. Mr. Anthony W. Ross, Mr.
David Merriweather, of Ogelthrope, Ga., to Miss Esther Ann Reese,
youngest daughter of Mr. George Reese, of this district.
Married on Tuesday the 15th ult., by the Rev. Mr. Manley, Mr. Oswald
Burt of Pendleton, to Miss Nancy Raiford, of Edgefield District.
Died on the 19th ult., at Centerville, Pendleton District, after
a long and painful illness, the Hon. Elias Earle, aged 61 years, late
member of Congress from the election district of Pendleton and Greenville.

Issue of June 11, 1823
Married on Thursday the 29th ult., by James Gaines, Esq., Mr. Reuben
Gains to Miss Mave Ann Evet, daughter of Mr. Lewis Evet, deceased, all
of this district.
Married on Tuesday the 3rd inst., by James C. Griffin, Esq., Mr.
Elias Madden, to Miss Mary Johns, all of this District.
Married in Charleston, on the 15th ult., by the Rev. Mr. Hanckel,
Col. A. Eustis, of the U. S. Army, to Miss Patience W. B. Izard, of
that place.

Issue of June 25, 1823
Died in Charleston, on the 2d inst., much lamented, Mr. John Dawson,
Cashier of the State Bank.
Died at Col. Griffin's, near Cambridge, S. C., Mr. Littleberry
Wilson, in the 53d year of his age.
Died in Charleston, on the morning of the 5th inst., in the 63d
year of his age, Gilbert Davidson, Esq., a native of Scotland, for the
last 40 years a highly respected and esteemed member of the community.
Died at his residence, near Winsborough, on the 18th ult., James
Barkley, Sen. in the 67th year of his age.
Died on the 7th ult., in St. Mathews Parish, Mr. Robert Caldwell,
in the 43d year of his age.

Issue of July 2, 1823
Married in Charleston on the 12th inst., Mr. Isaac Keith Holmes
of James Island to Miss Anna Maria Thayer. On the 15th inst., Stevens
Perry, Esq., to Melisant C. Jermyn, both of that city.
Died at Quincy, near Boston, on the 2d inst., Peter Boylston Adams
Esq., aged 85, brother of the late President of the U. S. In Charleston,
on the 3d inst., Major James M. Ward.

Issue of July 9, 1823
Maj. William Gustavus Gun was married at Petersburg (Vir.) on the
9th inst., to Miss Emily Maria Pistol, by the Rev. Mr. Cannon.

Issue of July 16, 1823

On Wednesday last, the house of Mr. William Mancel near Pickensville was struck by lightning, and his daughter Nancy Mancel, a girl of about 14 years of age was killed.

Married on Wednesday last, by the Rev. Joseph Hillhouse, Doctor Hugh McCann to Miss Rachel, youngest daughter of Col. Patrick Norris, all of this district.

Married by Edward Norton, Esq., on the 26th ult., Mr. Sidney Barr, to Miss Elizabeth Raines, all of this district.

Married on the 10th inst., by the Rev. Moses Holland, Mr. Halbert Acker of Pendleton District, to Miss Elizabeth, eldest daughter of Mr. Charles Garrison of Greenville District.

Died at Savannah, on the 23rd ult., in the 29th year of his age, Mr. William Darby, a native of South Carolina.

Died at New York, on the 14th ult., Mr. Richard Wells, formerly of this city.

Died at his residence near the Sweet Springs in Virginia, on the 4th inst., Capt. John Lewis, in the 68th year of his age, hero of the Revolution, and owner of the above celebrated Springs.

Issue of July 23, 1823

Correction in our last paper. Married on Wednesday the 9th inst., by the Rev. Wm. H. Barr, Doctor Hugh M'Cann, to Miss Rachel, youngest daughter of Col. Patrick Norris, all of this district.

Casualty--Drowned in the 23 mile Creek, on the 19th inst., William Madden, a youth of about 14 years of age.

Married on Wednesday the 16th inst., by the Rev. Moses Holland, Mr. William Mattison, to Miss Elizabeth Acker, eldest daughter of Mr. Peter Acker, deceased, all of this district.

Died of a Dropsey on Monday night 7th inst., Mrs. Elizabeth Dendy, aged 25 years, wife of Mr. J. H. Dendy, who with four children, are(sic) left to lament a loss to them irreparable.

Died on the 18th inst., Mrs. Mary Prater, aged 23 years, wife of Mr. John Prater of this district.

Died on the 1st inst., in Alabama, Mrs. Ldyia Martin, wife of Col. John Martin, formerly of this district.

Died in Charleston of Apoplexcy(sic), Samuel Colleton Graves, Esq., in the 35th year of his age.

Died at his residence on Pawley's Island, on Monday the 7th inst., the Hon. Benjamin Huger.

Died at Norfolk, on the 2d inst., Mrs. Elizabeth Barron, consort of Com. James Barron.

Issue of July 30, 1823

Died on Saturday last, by the bite of a spider, Mr. Tilman Saunders, aged 57 years.

Issue of August 27, 1823

Died on the 11th instant, in this village, Mrs. Ann Merriweather, aged 17 years, wife of Mr. David Merriweather, of Oglethorpe county, Georgia.

Issue of September 3, 1823

Died on the 26th instant at Greenville, S. C., Lieut. Caleb Lyman in the 33d year of his age, a native of Northfield, Massachusetts.

Issue of September 17, 1823

Married yesterday evening, by the Rev. Anthony Ross, Mr. Josia N. Boggs, to Miss Jane, eldest daughter of Mr. Crosby Wilkes Miller, all of this district.

Died on Friday last, Mrs. Frances Earle, relict of Elias Earle, deceased.

Died on the 29th August, Mr. Livingston Isbell, of this district.

Issue of October 1, 1823

Married on Tuesday the 23rd ult., by the Rev. Mr. Rector, Mr. Thomas Sloan, to Miss Ann, youngest daughter of Gen. John Blassingame of Greenville District.

Issue of October 8, 1823
    Married on the 30th ult., by the Rev. Mr. Calloway, Mr. Davis Hunt
of Greenville District, to Miss Harriot, only daughter of Mr. Benjamin
Perry of this district.

Issue of December 17, 1823
    Died in Pendleton District, Aug. 31, 1823, Mr. Arie Brown, aged
upwards of 70 years.
    Died on Saturday the 13th inst., at Col. John E. Calhoun's in the
54th year of her age, Mrs. Martha Davis, widow of the late Capt. William
Ransom Davis of the Revolutionary army.
    Died on the 31st ult., in Greenville District, Gen. John Blassingame
aged 54 years. (eulogy).
    Died near Marion, Perry County, on Wednesday the 15th ult., the
Rev. Andrew Brown, of the Presbyterian connection in the 59th year
of his age and the 34th year of his ministry.

Issue of January 7, 1824
    Married on Thursday last, by the Rev. Anthony W. Ross, Mr. Josiah D.
Gaillard, to Miss Ann Hamilton, daughter of Mr. Thomas Hamilton; all of
this district.
    Married on Thursday last, Mr. Joab Liddell, to Miss Sarah M'Clure,
daughter of Mr. Josiah M'Clure, all of this district.

Issue of January 14, 1824
    Died on the 9th inst., John Ewing, the infant son of Col. John E.
Colhoun, aged one year and three days.

Issue of January 21, 1824
    Married on Thursday, the 15th inst., by the Rev. William H. Barr,
the Rev. Anthony W. Ross, to Miss Elizabeth, second daughter of Mr.
Joseph Whitner, all of this district.

Issue of February 11, 1824
    Married on the 5th inst., by the Rev. Rodolphus Dickinson, Mr.
Samuel Gassaway, to Mrs. Ann Frances Hawes, all of this district.
    Died in this district, on the 3d inst., Mrs. Susan Humphreys, aged
24 years, wife of the Rev. David Humphreys, (eulogy).

Issue of February 25, 1824
    Obituary. The death of Gen. John Blassingame, which took place on
the 30th November, 1823, in the 55th year of his age, was an event which
must long be deplored by a numerous circle of acquaintances....a Member
of the S. C. Legislature...a short time before his death...had a wife
and six of seven children were married....

Issue of March 3, 1824
    Married on Sunday the 22d ult., by the Rev. Robert Gains, Mr. Jarred
Evatt, to Miss Margaret B., second daughter of James Gains, Esq., all of
this district.

Issue of March 10, 1824
    Married on the 5th inst., by David M'Kenney, Esq., Mr. Jordan M'Afee
to Miss Sarah, daughter of Mr. Anslem Roe, all of this district.
    Died on Sunday the 29th ult., Mrs. Jane Hamilton, wife of Mr. Wm.
Hamilton, of this district.

Issue of March 17, 1824
    Died on the evening of the 12th inst., Capt. Aaron Steele, of this
district, in the 31st year of his age--He has left a wife and two small
children....
    Died in Edgefield, on the 22d ult., Mrs. Eliza Glascock, widow of
the late Gen. Glascock, leaving five children....
    Died at Washington City, after a protracted illness, on the 1st
instant, the Hon. William Lee Ball, aged about 45, for several years
past, and at the time of his death, a Representative in Congress from
the State of Virginia.

Issue of March 24, 1824
  A horrible murder, says the Raleigh Register of Tuesday, was committed in Wake County on the 19th inst. The unfortunate victim was a Mrs. Collins....Fayetteville Observer.

Issue of March 31, 1824
  Died on Saturday last, Miss Mary M'Guffin, daughter of Mr. William M'Guffin, late of this district.

Issue of April 14, 1824
  Married in Greenwich, (Conn.), by the Rev. David Peck, Mr. Eliphalet Peck, jun. to Miss Deborah Peck.
  Died on Wednesday last, after a long and painful illness, which she bore with christian fortitude and resignation, Mrs. Mary Hunter, aged 64 years...member of the Presbyterian Church.
  Died on Thursday last, Mr. Joseph Morgan, aged 26. His death was occasioned by the falling of a limb from a dead tree....

Issue of April 21, 1824
  Died on Monday evening, the 12th inst., of Apoplexy, Mr. Joseph Whitner, aged 67 years. One amongst the most respectable and first inhabitants of this district...member of the Presbyterian Church....

Issue of April 28, 1824
  Married on Thursday, the 1st of April last, by the Rev. Levi Garrason, Mr. Isaac J. Foster, of Union District, to Miss Francis Stribling, daughter of Thomas Stribling, Esq., of this district.

Issue of May 12, 1824
  Married on Thursday the 29th ult., by the Rev. Moses Holland, Dr. George R. Brown to Miss Edney Broyles, daughter of Major Aaron Broyles, all of this district.

Issue of May 26, 1824
  Died at Mobile, on the 5th ult., Gen. Turner Starke, a native of South Carolina, but for some years a resident of Alabama, where he had acquired very great respect.

Issue of June 2, 1824
  Married on the 13th ultimo, Capt. George Reese, of Pendleton District, to Miss Mary Witherspoon, daughter of the late Mr. Gavin Witherspoon, of Williamburgh District, S. C.
  Died on the 25th ult., at his residence near this place, Major Joseph L. Steele, third son of William Steele, Esq., late of this district.

Issue of June 9, 1824
  Died on Thursday the 3d instant of Apoplexy, in the 46th year of his age, Mr. Thomas Lorton, well-known Inn-keeper at this village. (eulogy).

Issue of June 30, 1824
  Died on the 8th of March last, in the West of England, John Lee, Esquire, formerly a respectable merchant of Charleston, and for many years Postmaster at Bachelors Retreat, in this district...in the 57th year of his age.

Issue of July 21, 1824
  Married on Thursday last, by James Gains, Esq., Mr. Matthew Mullenix, to Miss Dorothy Canada, youngest daughter of Wm. Arnold, sen., all of this district.

Issue of July 28, 1824
  Died at his residence in this district, on the 15th instant, Mr. Laurens M'Gregory, aged 54 (eulogy).

Issue of August 18, 1824
  Died on Monday the 9th inst., Miss Sarah Graham, aged 16 years, daughter of Mr. William Graham, of this district.
  Married on Thursday, the 12th instant, by James Garvin, Esq., Mr. Jesse Evatt to Miss Rebecca Gassaway, daughter of Mr. Nicholas Gassaway.

Issue of September 1, 1824
    Married on Tuesday the 10th ult., by the Rev. Joseph Hillhouse,
Mr. Emeriah Fulton to Miss Nancy Brown, all of this district.

Issue of September 8, 1824
    Died on Monday evening, the 16th last at his residence in Lower
Marion Township, Montgomery County, Pennsylvania, Charles Thompson,
Esq., in the 95th year of his age. Secretary of the Continental
Congress.
    In Franklin county, Missouri, on the night of the 6th ult., Joseph
Jones Monroe, Esq. (brother of the President of the United Stated.).

Issue of September 22, 1824
    Married on Thursday evening the 16th inst., by the Rev. Rodolphus
Dickinson, Doctor William Anderson, to the amiable Miss Mary Hunter,
daughter of Mr. Thomas Hunter, all of this village.
    Married yesterday evening, by the Rev. Rodolphus Dickinson, Jesse P.
Lewis, Esq., of this village to Miss Susan, eldest daughter of Col.
Joseph Taylor, all of this district.

Issue of November 3, 1824
    Died, Departed this life on Friday the 22nd ult., Mr. Robert
Looney, aged 75 years, leaving a numerous connexion...By his death,
the heroes of 76 have lost a brother...(eulogy).

Issue of November 10, 1824
    Married on Tuesday the 9th inst., by the Rev. Anthony W. Ross, Mr.
Charles Miller, to Miss Rebecca Hamilton, daughter of Mr. Thomas
Hamilton, all of this district.
    Married on Thursday, the 4th inst., by James C. Griffin, Esq., Mr.
George A. Kitchens, to Miss Ann Mitchell, daughter of Mr. Joseph Mit-
chell, all of this district.

Issue of November 17, 1824
    Obituary. Departed this life on the 27th ult., in the 82nd year of
his age, at his residence in Union, Mr. Samuel Clowney, after a severe
illness of nine months. He was a native of Ireland--came to this country while colonies of Great Britain...has been upwards of 60 years a
citizen of Carolina. In the struggle for independence, he was an active
soldier. When South-Carolina was overrun with the enemy, and the hope
of liberty was almost extinct, he was one of the few who met in North
Carolina, chose the gallant Sumter for their leader...fought as a
volunteer under Brandon, Williams, Sumpter and Morgan...none but the
partner of his bosom and an affectionate offspring can estimate his loss.

Issue of December 29, 1824
    Married on Tuesday the 21st instant, by the Rev. Anthony W. Ross,
Mr. James M. Orr, to Miss Mary Dickson, daughter of Mr. James Dickson,
deceased, all of this district.

Issue of January 26, 1825
    Married on the 2nd instant, by the Rev. Benjamin DuPre, Mr. William
Henry Adair, to Miss Nancy Blackburn.
    Married on the 18th, by the same, Mr. John Dickson, jun. to Miss
Lititia, daughter of Mr. Jonathan Smith.
    Married on the 13th inst., by A. J. Liddell, Esq., Mr. Reuben West
to Miss Dianna Madden, all of this distirct.

Issue of February 9, 1825
    Died, Suddenly, on the 14th ult., about nine o'clock, after eating
breakfast as usual with his family, Robert Goodloe Harper, Esq., of
Baltimore...for more than two weeks past Gen. Harper had been actively
and anxiously engaged in the trial of an important cause in the Circuit
Court of the U. S. for the Dist. of Maryland...he was sixty years of
age.

Issue of February 23, 1825
    Married on the 17th inst., by Nathan Boon, Esq., Mr. Robert Craig
to Miss Rachael Speed, daughter of William Speed, Esq., all of this
district.

Issue of March 9, 1825
 Married on the 13th Feb. last, by John T. Lewis, Esq., Mr. Ashby
Owens to Miss Hannah Farmer. On the 3d March, by the same, Mr. Linden
King to Miss Nancy Hughes, all of this district.
 Married on Thursday the 3d instant, by the Rev. Anthony W. Ross, Mr.
George Miller, to Miss Cynthia T. Hamilton, youngest daughter of Mr.
Thomas Hamilton, all of this district.
 Died on the 6th January last, after a short illness, at his residence
on Pacolett, in Spartanburgh district, Baylis Earle, in the 91st year
of his age. He came to this State from Virginia, about the commencement
of the Revolutionary War...About the year 1770, in Virginia, he became
a member of the Baptist Church. (long eulogy).

Issue of April 20, 1825
 Murder. Another horris murder was committed in Edgefield District,
on the evening of the 22d ult., upon Peter Morgan, who resided near the
junction of Turkey and Steven's Creek. The horris deed was committed
by Alexander Howl, son-in-law to the deceased...Mr. Morgan stood high
among his neighbours, he was one of the survivors of the Revoluionary
War, and was at the siege of York, when Cornwallis was captured.
From the South Carolina Republican.

Issue of May 18, 1825
 Married on Thursday the 12th inst., by the Rev. Anthony W. Ross, Mr.
William Hamilton, to Miss Martha Lemon, daughter of Mr. Robert Lemon,
all of this district.

Issue of May 25, 1825
 Died on Monday evening last, in this village, Mr. Thomas Hunter,
aged 60 years...left an affectionate widow and two children.

Issue of June 1, 1825
 Died on Saturday the 7th ult., of pulmonary consumption, Miss
Catharine Barry, only daughter of the late Wm. T. Barry, deceased,
aged about 16 years. And on Tuesday the 24th after a long illness,
her mother, Mrs. Nancy Barry aged 38 (eulogy).

Issue of June 15, 1825
 From the Hamburg Gazette. Horrid Murder!!! On Saturday the 22d
ultimo, a man by the name of Gunnels, of this district, was murdered
by his step brother, Aaron Carter, while asleep.

Issue of June 22, 1825
 Died in this district, on the 7 ult., of a lingering illness,
Ebenezer Stuart Dickson, youngest son of Benjamin Dickson, Esq. (eulogy).

Issue of July 13, 1825
 A negro fellow named William,the property of Mr. Cokergee, of the
State of Georgia, was found guilty of the murder of Mr. Peter Garrison,
late of Greenville district....

Issue of November 9, 1825
 Married on Sunday the 6th inst., by the Rev. Sandford Vandivere,
Major Thomas Benson, of Greenville, to Mrs. Catharine Stribling, of
this district.

Issue of November 23, 1825
 Married on the 6th inst., at the house of the Widow Bradford,
Greenville District, by the Rev. Mr. Jordon, William Grisham, Esq.,
of Decater, DeKealb County, Georgia, formerly of Pendleton District,
to Miss Susan Bradford, daughter of the late Philemon Bradford.
 Died at Pensacola, on the 25th ult., John Simpson, Esq., late
of this district; he moved with his family to Pensacola, soon after the
acquisition of the Floridas. He left a wife and large family of
children...raised in this district.

Issue of December 14, 1825
 Died on Wednesday last, Mr. Albert Whitten; the deceased came to his
death by a fall from a horse...left a wife and one child, a father and
mother, brothers and sisters.

Issue of February 8, 1826

Married on Tuesday the 21st ult., by Rev. Sandford Vandiver, Mr. Andrew N. McFall to Miss Rachel Thompson, daughter of Capt. James Thompson, of this district.

Died on the 28th ult., Mrs. Martha Duncan, wife of Mr. Hugh Duncan of this district. She emigrated from Ireland in 1790 and has remained in this District almost ever since. Her descendants were 9 children, 66 grandchildren, and 63 great-grandchildren.

Issue of February 15, 1826

Married on the 26th ult., by Rev. Sanford Vandiver, Mr. Abner Magee of Abbeville to Miss Louisa, daughter of Mr. Hezekiah Rice of this district.

Married on Thursday the 2nd inst., by Rev. Mr. Arnold, Mr. Powel Gains of Laurens, to Miss Nancy, eldest daughter of Capt. Robert B. Norris of this District.

Married on Tuesday the 7th by Robert M'Cann, Mr. John P. Archer to Miss Melinda, daughter of Maj. Andrew Hamilton, all of this District.

Married on Wednesday evening last, by John C. Anderson, Esq., Mr. Jason Howard to Miss Matilda, daughter of Mr. Howard Duckworth, of this district.

Issue of February 22, 1826

Died at Edgefield Village on the 2d inst., Edmund Bacon, Esq. (long eulogy).

Issue of March 1, 1826

Married in the village of Greenville, on Tuesday evening, the 21st ult., by Rev. Mr. Johnson, Miss Mary, eldest daughter of Col. William Toney to Mr. Tandy Walker.

Issue of March 22, 1826

We are sorry to have to announce the death of Mr. John E. Norris of Small-pox. Mr. Norris was a high respectable man...left a wife and a family of small children....

Died at his residence in this district, on the 9th inst., Col. Elias Moore Sen., in the 75th year of his age. He was born in Augusta Cy., near Stanton, Va....came to this state when a lad and settled with the family near Cambridge. the interest which he and his brother Samuel took in favor of the Revolution ought to make the name of Moore dear to the sons and daughters of freedom...left widow and children.

Issue of March 29, 1826

Died on Tuesday the 21st inst., Mr. Alexander Ramsay sen., aged 79...

Died on Saturday evening, of small pox, Mr. John Curtis, aged about 25 years.

Issue of April 5, 1826

Married on the 15th ult., by Micajah Gaut, Esq., Mr. Samuel J. Lee of Pendleton District, to Miss Ann McKinney, of Abbeville District.

Died on Wednesday last, Mr. Naaman Curtis, of Small Fox, aged about 45 years, for many years a respectable inhabitant of this district.

Died on Saturday morning last, the Rev. Jeremiah Winter, aged 43 years. He was a native of England, but for the last ten years, a resident of this district...member of the Methodist church. A funeral service will be preached at his late residence on Sunday next by the Rev. Green W. Huckaby.

Issue of April 26, 1826

Died on the 4th inst., Mr. John Taylor, aged 21 years, a student of the Pendleton Academy, and son of Mr. Champ Taylor of this district.

Died on Saturday evening last, after a long illness, Mr. Benjamin Lawrence, aged 79 years. Mr. Lawrence was actively engaged in the cause of liberty during the war of independence...member of the Baptist church.

Issue of May 10, 1826

Died on Saturday evening last, Mr. Frederic Johnson, an old and respectable inhabitant of this district.

Died on Sunday morning at his residence in this district, Mr. Thomas

K. Edwards, formerly of Charleston.

Issue of May 17, 1826
Married on Thursday evening last, by the Rev. Anthony W. Ross, Mr.
William Smith of Georgetown, to Miss Sarah, only daughter of Mr. Benjamin
Smith of this District.

Issue of June 23, 1826
Died on Saturday evening the 17th inst., Mrs. Anna F. Reese, aged
34 years, wife of Dr. Charles M. Reese of this Village.

Issue of July 12, 1826
Died on Thursday the 22d ult., after a long and painful illness, Mr.
John Barry, aged about 40 years. He was a native of Virginia, but for
many years a respectable inhabitant of this district...has left a widow
and several small children.
Died at the residence of her father on the Beaverdam in this District
on the 2d inst., Miss Maria, second daughter of Capt. Wm. B. Hull, aged
near 11 years.

Issue of August 9, 1826
Married on Thursday evening last by the Rev. Anthony W. Ross, Mr.
Samuel B. Fickens of Alabama, to Miss Martha T Anderson, eldest daughter
of Col. Robert Anderson of this district.

Issue of August 23, 1826
The venerable Isaac Shelby, another distinguished Revolutionary
Patriot and Statesman, is gone. He died at his residence in Lincoln
county on the 19th ultimo.
Col. Shelby was the first Governor of Kentucky, and was called a sec-
ond time to that office. He acted a conspicuous part in the battle of
Kings Mountain during the Revolution, as well as the battle of Thomas,
in Upper Canada, in the last war. Ken. Gazette.

Issue of August 30, 1826
Married in Trinity Church, New Haven, Conn. on Sunday evening the 13th
inst., by the Rev. Mr. Croswell, Mr. Jabez B. Bull of this place, to Miss
Polly Ford, of that City.
Died in the 24th year of his age, in the neighborhood of Petersburg,
Elbert County, Ga., on the 10th instant, Dr. William W. Acker, after an
illness of 11 days. He was buried in the Town of Petersburg, a stranger
in a strange land.
Dr. Acker was born and raised on Saluda River, in Pendleton district,
South Carolina. He left his father in the beginning of 1821, and went to
reside with a friend and relation in Franklin County, Ga., in the the
beginning of 1822 he resolved on studying Medicine..

Issue of September 20, 1826
Died in the Village of Greenville, on Thursday the 14th inst., after
a short illness, Mr. Alexander Sloan, in the 40th year of his age...left
a wife and four young children....

Issue of September 27, 1826
Married on Thursday evening last by the Rev. Mr. Dickinson, Mr. David
S. Taylor to Miss Lucy Anna, second daughter of Zacharias Taliaferro, Esq.,
all of this district.
Married on the same evening, by Jas. C. Griffin, Esq., Mr. William P.
Dennis, to Miss Rhoda Eppes, all of this district.
Died at New-York, on the 7th instant, the Hon. William P. Van Ness,
U. S. District Judge for the Southern district of New-York.
Died on the same day, in Queen Anne County, Maryland, the Hon. Robert
Wright, Associate Judge of the second Judicial district of that state.
He was formerly Governor of Maryland.
Died at Carthagena, on the 7th July, in the 25th year of his age,
William Barrien, Esq., Vice Consul of the U. S. at that port, formerly of
Philadelphia.

Issue of October 18, 1826
    Died at his late residence in this place, on the 4th inst., Mr. John
Miller sen. former editor of the Pendleton Messenger, in the 56th year of
his age, leaving a large family.
    Died on Monday evening last, Capt. David Sloan sen., aged 74 years.
A native of Ireland, he emigrated to America in early youth and was engaged
in the struggle for independence.
    Died on Saturday last, suddenly, Mr. Thomas Carey, aged upwards of 70
years, a very old and well-known inhabitant of this district.

Issue of October 25, 1826
    Married on Thursday the 19th inst., by Rev. James Hembree, Mr. Robert
W. Reeves to Eliza Jane, second daughter of A. J. Liddell, all of this
district.

Issue of November 8, 1826
    Married on Thursday evening last by James Osborn, Esq., Mr. Joseph
Taylor to Miss Lucinda, daughter of Edward Norton, Esq.
    Married on the 31st October by Rev. David Humphreys, Major James
Gilmer to Miss Elizabeth Colhoun.
    Married on the same evening, Elias Dendy to Miss Feriby Wimby of this
District.
    Married on Thursday the 2d inst., by Hugh Gaston, Esq., Mr. David Welch
of Habersham, Geo., to Miss Elizabeth, eldest daughter of Mr. Ephraim
Robinson, of this district.
    Died on the 28th ult., Mr. Daniel Bates, aged 71 years, a Revolutionary
soldier and an honest man.
    Died at his residence on Edisto Island, on the evening of the 17th ult.,
Isaac Auld, M. D. Hon. member of the Medical Society of South Carolina
in the 57th year of his age.
    Died at Boston, on the 13th ult., the venerable John Tileston, in the
92nd year of his age, for many years Master of the North Writing school
in that city.

Issue of November 15, 1826
    Died on Tuesday the 7th inst., near Greenville C. H., Capt. William
Young, in the 67th year of his age. He was a Revolutionary patriot...
(eulogy).

Issue of November 22, 1826
    Married on the 15th inst., by Rev. Henry Reid, Dr. John S. Reid to Mrs.
Anna Eliza Norris, all of Abbeville District.

Issue of January 17, 1827
    Married on the 4th inst., by Rev. Francis Callaway, Mr. Thomas J. Rusk
to Miss Mary F., eldest daughter of Gen. Benjamin Cleveland, all of Haber-
sham County, Ga.
    Married on Thursday last, Mr. John Donaldson to Miss Nancy, daughter of
Mr. Isaac Thomas, all of this District.
    Married on Tuesday evening by Rev. Benjamin D. DuPre, Mr. John W. M.
Blassingame of Greenville, to Miss Sarah, eldest daughter of Capt. David
Sloan of this District.

Issue of January 24, 1827
    Married on the 2nd inst., by Rev. D. C. DuPre, Mr. Alexander Brice to
Miss Jane Toms, all of this District.
    Married on the18th inst., by Rev. D. Humphreys of Pendleton, John W.
Hooper Esq., of Ga., to Miss Sarah A. Word, daughter of Col. Word, of
Laurens, S. C.

Issue of February 7, 1827
    Married yesterday evening by J. C. Griffin, Esq., Mr. William Faton to
Miss Zelia, eldest daughter of Mr. Thomas Davis, all of this district.
    Married on 30 January by Rev. D. Humphreys, Mr. Chas. Hany to Miss
Nancy Reid, both of this District.
    Married on 1 February by the same, Mr. Thomas M'Alister, to Miss Mar-
garet M'Keown, both of Abbeville District.

Issue of February 21, 1827
    Married on 23d January last, by Rev. Robert Gaines, Mr. Matthew Knox

to Miss Melinda Nicholson, all of this district.
    Married on the 6th inst., by William Beavert, Esq., Mr. Martin Moss
to Miss Drusilla Norton, all of this district.

Issue of February 28, 1827
    Married on Thursday the 22d inst., by Henry Freeman, Esq., Mr. Alvin
E. Whitten to Miss Catherine Whiting Jones, all of Carnesville, Ga.

Issue of March 28, 1827
    Married yesterday evening by Rev. B. D. DuPre, Mr. George W. Liddell
to Miss Rebecca, eldest daughter of Mr. Andrew Harris, all of this district.
    Married on Tuesday the 20th inst., by the same, Mr. Cornelius P. Dupre
to Miss Mary E., second daughter of Mr. Thomas W. Carne, all of this
district.
    Married on the 15th inst., by Rev. Mr. Hilliard, Mr. John Hallum, of
this district, to Miss Francis, daughter of Capt. William Hamilton of
Clarkesville, Ga.

Issue of May 2, 1827
    Married on Thursday evening last, Mr. John B. Prator to Miss Eliza Ann,
daughter of Mr. Richard Hallum, all of this District.
    Died on Wednesday last, Capt. William Perkins, an old inhabitant of
this district.

Issue of May 9, 1827
    Married yesterday evening by the Rev. Mr. Dickinson, John H. Goodlett
Esq., of Greenville, to Miss Sarah Catherine M'Gregor, of this district.
    Died on Thursday last, Mrs. Sarah Prator, wife of Mr. John Prator, of
this district.

Issue of June 13, 1827
    Died on the 23d April last, near Matanzas, where he had gone for the
benefit of his health, Israel Pickens, late Gov. of Alabama.
    Died at Boston, on the 25th ult., the Hon. William Phillips, late Lt.
Gov. of Massachusetts, aged 77 years.

Issue of June 20, 1827
    Married on the 15th inst., by Nathan Boon, Esq., Mr. Parks Strawhorn
to Miss Eliza,daughter of the widow Spillars, all of this district.
    Died on Thursday evening last,Mr. Josiah Wright, aged about 50 years,
an honest and industrious man.
    Died about 10 days since of consumption, Mr. Elijah Sprigg, aged 26.

Issue of June 27, 1827
    Died on Wednesday evening last, Mr. Jonathan West, a resident of this
District.
    Died on Saturday evening last in this place, Mr. James Forrest.
    Died at his residence in Spartanburg District, on Thursday, the 31st
ult., in the 38th year of his age, Dr. Hugh Davitt, for many years an
eminent practising physician of Unionville, S. C.
    Died at Clarksville, Habersham Co., Ga., on Wednesday 20 June, James
Maulden, aged 2 years and 9 months. On Sunday the 24th, Samuel Wales, aged
11 months, only children of James and Sarah Hodges.

Issue of July 11, 1827
    Died on Saturday evening last, at the house of Mr. Steele in this place,
Mrs. Caroline B. O'Riley, late from Charleston(widow), in the 39th year of
her age.
    Died at the house of Mrs. Kyle near Abbeville C. H. , on the evening
of the 6th inst., Martha Jane Grisham, eldest daughter of Col. Jos.
Grisham of this place, having just attained her 13th year.
    Died at Tallahassee on the 12th ult., Hon. Augustus B. Woodard, Judge
of the Supreme Court for Middle Florida.
    Died on the 20th ult., in New-York, whither he had gone for the bene-
fit of his health, Thos. Worthington of Ohio...for many years a Senator
of the U. S. from Ohio and a subsequent Governor of that State.

Issue of July 18, 1827
    We learn that Maj. Gen. Thomas Carr died at Georgetown, S. C. on Friday
last. Char. Mercury.

26

Issue of July 25, 1827
Died on the 22d inst., after a protracted and painful illness, Eliza-
beth Joudon, wife of Isaac Joudon of this district....leaving a husband and
4 children.
Died near this place, on the 18th inst., Mr. Julius H. Walker, of
Wilmington, N. C. aged about 33 years.

Issue of August 15, 1827
Married at Winsborough by the Rev. Mr. Rennie, the Rev. Richard B.
Cater of Abbeville, to Miss Jemima M., daughter of Rev. Samuel W. Yongue.

Issue of August 22, 1827
Married on Thursday the 16th inst., by Rev. Mr. Boring, Mr. John W.
Gasaway to Miss Sarah M'Dow, both of this district.
Died on Thursday the 9th inst., aged 41 years, Mrs. Elizabeth, consort
of Mr. Thomas Johnston of Charleston, formerly of this district.

Issue of August 29, 1827
Died on Thursday last, Mrs. Susan Cooper, wife of James Cooper, Esq.,
aged about 60 years.

Issue of September 19, 1827
Married on Sunday evening last, by James C. Griffin, Esq., Mr. Elias
Roberts to Miss Dursilla Edmonson, all of this village.
Died in this place on Sunday last, the 16th inst., Dr. Henry W. Davis,
in the 32nd year of his age...graduated from S. C. College in 1811 and
pursued medicine under Dr. Edward Fisher of Columbia...(account of life
and eulogy).

Issue of September 26, 1827
The death of Mathew Talbot of Georgia...died 17th inst....of Wilkes
County.

Issue of October 10, 1827
Died on the 27th ult., Mrs. ____ Whitten, wife of Mr. Charles Whitten,
of this district.
Died on Wednesday last, Mr. Matthew Mullinax. His death was supposed
to have been caused by a fall from his horse some weeks previous.
Died on Saturday last, Mr. Thos Wallace Hamilton, in the 27th year of
his age...leaves aged parents, a sister and three orphan children.
Died in Abbeville District, on the 20th ult., Maj. John Bowie, a soldier of the Revolution.

Issue of October 24, 1827
Married on the 16th inst., by Rev. Mr. Vandiver, Mr. H. S. Linton of
Abbeville, to Miss Emily Benson, of this district.
Married on the same day, by the Rev. James Hembree, Mr. James Yeatin to
Miss Minerva Mayhon, all of this district.
Died on Genorostee, on Monday last, Capt. William M'Gregor...and in
the same neighborhood, Mr. Jonathan Watson, both respectable citizens of
this district.

Issue of November 7, 1827
Married at Edgefield C. H., S. C. on the evening of the 18th ult., by
the Rev. Mr. Warne, Mr. Francis W. Pickens of Alabama, to Miss Margaret
Eliza, eldest daughter of Col. Eldred Simkins.
Died on the 31st ult., Warren Davis, youngest son of Hugh Gaston, aged
3 years.
Died in Twinsburg, Portage Co., Ohio, on the 21st ult., Moses and Aaron
Wilcox, aged about 50 years...they were twin brothers, b. in Connecticut,
on the same day. Their wives were sisters....Cleveland Herald.

Issue of November 14, 1827
Died on the 5th inst., John George Esq., aged 77 years an inhabitant
of this district 28 years and a ruling elder in the Associate Reformed
Church...left a widow and several children.

Issue of November 28, 1827
Married in Greenville on Tuesday, the 20th inst., by the Rev. W. R.
Johnson, Dr. William Robinson, to Miss Maria, second daughter of the late

George W. Earle, Esq., all of Greenville District.

Issue of December 12, 1827
Married on the 2d inst., by James C. Griffin, Esq., Mr. Thomas Dodd to Miss Catherine, eldest daughter of Mr. William Hunnicutt.
Married on the 27th ult., by the Rev. W. B. Johnson, Mr. O. H. Wells publisher of the Greenville Republican to Miss Amelia Headden, all of Greenville District.

Issue of December 19, 1827
Died on Monday the 17th inst., Miss Sarah Ann, daughter of Mr. William Brewster, aged 12 years and 1 month.
Also on Tuesday the 8th inst., Mrs. Margaret Brewster, mother to the young lady who died on the day previous...left a husband and large family of children.

Issue of February 6, 1828
Married on Thursday evening the 31st ultimo, by John T. Lewis, David Moore Jun., to the amiable Miss Fanny Elrod, all of this district.

Issue of February 13, 1828
Married on the 5th instant, Mr. Willis Geer to Miss Cynthia, daughter of Mr. Joseph Hull. On the same day, Mr. Thomas Hanks, to Miss Elizabeth, daughter of Mr. Thomas W. Means, sen. On the 3d inst., by Wm. Swords, Esq., Mr. Russell Shipley, to Miss Lydia Prator. On the 31st ult., by the Rev. Mr. Vandiver, Mr. Samuel M'Querne to Miss Caroline Keys. On the 29th ult., by James Osborne, Esq., Mr. Dobson Warnock to Miss Sarah Emberson, all of this district.

Issue of February 20, 1828
Married on Thursday last by the Rev. Mr. Crowther, Mr. Samuel Stark of Abbeville to Miss Rosa, daughter of Mr. Jesse Rutledge of this district.
Married on Thursday last, by Rev. Sanford Vandiver, Mr. Britain Haney to Miss Lotta Johnson.

Issue of March 5, 1828
Died on Thursday evening last, the 28th ult., after a very long and tedious illness, Mr. Daniel Symmes, in the 67th year of his age...a native of Andover, Mass., but for 30 years a resident of this district.

Issue of March 12, 1828
Married on the 4th inst., by Rev. S. Vandiver, Mr. Joseph Brown to Miss Mary, daughter of Capt. Samuel Moore.
Married on the 7th by Brian Burrows, Esq., Mr. Robert L. Robertson, to Miss Rachel S. Williams.

Issue of March 19, 1828
Married on Wednesday the 12th inst., by the Rev. H. Reid, in Abbeville District, Maj. Armistead Burt, of this place, to Miss Martha Catherine, second daughter of Mr. William Calhoun, of the former place.
Married on Tuesday the 18th inst., by the Rev. S. Vandiver, Mr. Elijah Webb to Miss Caroline Hammond, all of this district.
Died at her residence near Franklin, Haywood Co., N. C., on the evening of 18 February, Mrs. Caroline Hall, wife of Mr. John Hall, late of this place...leaves a husband and 4 small children...member of the Presbyterian Church.

Issue of March 26, 1828
Married on Thursday evening, the 20th inst., by John T. Lewis, Esq., Mr. William Owens to Miss Jane Golding.
Married on Friday evening, the 21st inst., by the same, Mr. Anthony Moore to Miss Eliza.Day, all of Anderson District.

Issue of April 9, 1828
Married on Thursday last, by James Gaines, Esq., Mr. Isaac Judon to Miss Martha Mitchell, all of Pickens District.
Married on the 19th ult., by Bryan Burniss, Esq., Mr. Joseph Drennan to Miss Phoebe H. Norris, both of the village of Anderson.
Married on the 20th ult., by Rev. S. Vandiver, Mr. Reuben Burriss, to Miss Delilah Burriss, both of Anderson District.

28

Issue of May 6, 1828
Died on the 3d instant, Master Billy William Fretwell, aged 5 years, son of Mr. John Fretwell, of Anderson District.

Issue of May 14, 1828
Died at Washington City on the 2d inst., Thomas Tudor Tucker, Esq., Treasurer of the U. S....in the 84th year of his age...He was a representative in the first Congress from S. C.
Died on Tuesday the 29th ult., at Sandy River, Chester District, Mr. William Hall, a native of Scotland.

Issue of May 21, 1828
Married on Tuesday the 13th inst., by the Rev. Francis Callaway, Mr. William D. Sloan to Miss Martha, daughter of Mr. Jabez Jones, all of Pickens District.
Married on the 13th inst., by the Rev. S. Vandiver, Mr. David R. Brazeel of Anderson District, to Miss Utinsy W., daughter of Mr. Silas Holloway, all of Greenville District.

Issue of June 11, 1828
Married on Thursday evening last, by the Rev. A. W. Ross, Mr. John F. Max of Charleston, to Miss Eliza Adams, daughter of Mr. John Adams.

Issue of July 2, 1828
Married in Anderson District, on Tuesday the 24th ult., by the Rev. Mr. Holland, Maj. George Seaborn of Greenville District, to Miss Sarah Ann, daughter of Gen. J. B. Earle, of the former district.

Issue of July 9, 1828
Married on yesterday evening by the Rev. Mr. Foster, Mr. Joseph F. Miller to Miss Anne R., daughter of Mr. C. W. Miller, all of this district.

Issue of July 16, 1828
Married on Wednesday evening last, by the Rev. Mr. Ross, Mr. Madison C. Livingston of Hamburg to Miss Anamina, eldest daughter of Ira Griffin, Esq., of this village.

Issue of July 23, 1828
Married on Tuesday the 15th inst., by the Rev. Mr. Humphreys, Dr. Edmund Webb to Miss Martha Ann Amberson, all of Anderson District.
Died on the morning of the 16th inst., after a few days illness, Rebecca Mary, youngest daughter of Rev. A. W. Ross, aged 11 months and 8 days.

Issue of July 30, 1828
Died on 5 June last, Mr. John Knox, aged 64 years. He was a native of Ireland, but for many years a respectable inhabitant of Pendleton district.
Married on Thursday evening last by Rev. Mr. Ross, Mr. Jos. C. Eaton to Miss Jane Robinson, daughter of Mr. Ephraim Robinson, all of Anderson district.
Married on Tuesday the 22d inst., by James C. Griffin, Esq., Mr. Loton Davis to Miss Mary M'Kenzie, all of Anderson.

Issue of August 13, 1828
Married on Tuesday the 31st July by the Rev. S. Vandiver, Mr. James Hawthorn of Abbeville District, to Miss Louisa, daughter of Mr. Jesse Rutledge of Anderson District.
Married on Tuesday the 5th August by the Rev. S. Vandiver, Dr. Stephen Holloway, to Miss Maria, daughter of Col. C. Garrison, both of Greenville District.
Died on the 5th August, Mrs. Rebecca Hamilton, wife of Mr. Luke Hamilton...left a husband and many relations.

Issue of August 20, 1828
Married on the 5th inst., by Rev. Charles Durham, Mr. Larkin Gambrell, to Miss Susannah Elenor, daughter of Rev. James Douthit, all of this district.

Issue of August 27, 1828
Died on Monday last, Mrs. Harriet Earle, wife of Samuel Earle of this district, aged about 49 years...leaves a husband and a large family of children.

Issue of October 1, 1828

Married on the 23d ult., by Rev. Sanford Vandiver, Mr. Noah Archer, of Anderson Village, to Miss Hannah Bailey, daughter of Mr. Robert Bailey.

Married on the 25th ult., by the same, Mr. Peter Johnson to Miss Nancy, daughter of Mr. Archibald Nichols, both of Anderson district.

Married on Sunday the 14th ult., by the same, Mr. Francis Miller, to Miss Rebecca Goff, both of Laurens District.

Issue of November 5, 1828

Married on the 28th ult., by Rev. Benjamin D. Dupre, Mr. Benjamin Kilpatrick to Miss Rebecca C., daughter of Mr. Jesse Stribling, all of Pickens District.

Married on the 30th ult., by Rev. Aaron Foster, Mr. William Noble to Miss Caroline, daughter of Alexander Houston, Esq., all of Abbeville District.

Died at his residence on Keowee River, near Pickens C. H., on the 10th ult., Jos. Reid, Esq., in the 72d year of his age...one of the Revolutionary Patriots and one of the first settlers in that part of the country...left a wife and 9 children.

Died near Carnesville, Geo., on the 30th of September last, Mrs. Frances Hammond, wife of Capt. William Hammond, aged 28 years, 5 months and 9 days. She had been married 10 years, 5 months and 20 days. She left 6 children---the oldest aged 9 years and seven months, the youngest, 9 months...about three years a member of the Methodist Episcopal Church.

Issue of November 12, 1828

Died at his residence near this place on Friday night, Mr. Lewis L. Gibbes, formerly of Charleston.

Issue of November 19, 1828

Died on Thursday night last, Mr. Alexander Bryce, an old and respectable inhabitant of this District.

Died on Monday morning, Mr. John Bishop, aged about 30 years, a native of this district.

Died on Thursday night, Mrs. _____ Brownlow, wife of John Brownlow, Sr.

Issue of November 26, 1828

Married on the 18th inst., by the Rev. S. Vandiver, Mr. Williamson Brazeal to Miss Penelope H. Holloway of Greenville District.

Married at Hamburg, S. C., on Tuesday evening the 18th inst., by Rev. Hugh Smith, Dr. Lewis D. Ford of Augusta to Miss Frances Emily,Chiles, daughter of John Chiles, deceased.

Died on the 18th inst., Mrs. Jane Dalton, wife of Mr. John Dalton of this district...left a husband and infant child.

Issue of December 3, 1828

Died in Haywood Co., N. C. on the evening of the 27 of November, Lt. Samuel Wragg of the U. S. Army and graduate of the Military Academy... interred in the Episcopal Church-yard at this place on the 30th...a meritorious stranger who died in his country's service.

Issue of December 10, 1828

Married on Tuesday the 4th inst., by the Rev. S. Vandiver, Mr. Hezekiah Pice to Miss Jane Todd, both of Anderson District.

Married on Thursday the 13th ult., by the same, Mr. William Armstrong of Abbeville district to Miss Elizabeth Roberts of Anderson District.

Married on the 13th ult., by the same, Mr. Allen M'David of Greenville District to Miss Theresa Acker of Anderson District.

Issue of December 31, 1828

Married on Thursday the 18th inst., by the Rev. S. Vandiver, Mr. Elijah Griffin to Miss Margaret M'Coy...both of this district.

Married on the 25th inst., by the same, Mr. Josiah Harper to Miss Mary H. Townes,both of this district.

Married on the 25th inst., by Thomas Lamar, Esq., Mr. George W. Adair of Pickens District, to Miss Eleanor, daughter of Henry Whitmire of Buncombe.

Issue of January 7, 1829

Married on the 30th ult., by Rev. S. Vandiver, Mr. William R. Jones to Miss Elenor, daughter of Capt. Adam Todd, all of Anderson District.

30

Died in Abbeville district, on the 10th november last, Mrs. Caroline M. M'Querns, aged 18 years.

Issue of January 14, 1829
Died suddenly on Friday evening last, Dr. George Hall...formerly a reputable physician of Charleston, and for the last nine years, a respectable inhabitant of this district.
Died on Saturday last, Mr. Abner Crosby, aged about 40 years, a native of Pendleton.

Issue of January 21, 1829
Married on Thursday the 6th inst., by Rev. S. Vandiver, Mr. David Gortney to Miss Margery Long, both of Anderson district.
Married on the 6th inst., by Rev. Wm. W. Belcher, Mr. William Walker to Miss Mary Ann Tullis, both of Abbeville district.
Married on the 11th inst., by Bryan Borroughs, Esq., Mr. William Master to Miss Edy Johnson, both of Anderson District.
Married on the 13th inst., by James Gunnin, Esq., Mr. John Tippins to Miss Eliza Castlebury, both of Anderson District.
Married on the 15th inst., by James Gunnin, Esq., Mr. James Cain, to Miss Hetty Skelton, both of Anderson District.
Married on the 8th inst., by Rev. Mr. Carr, Mr. Thomas P(?) Lamar to Miss Mary Ellis, both of Pickens District.
Married on the 30th ult., by Rev. George Vandiver, Mr. Peter Barton to Miss Nancy Terrill, both of ᵖickens District.

Issue of February 4, 1829
Married on the 28th ult., by Wm. L. Keith, Esq., Mr. Benjamin Morgan to Miss A. Barton, all of Pickens District.
Married on the 21st ult., by the Rev. G. Vandiver, Mr. George Colhoun to Miss Ruth Barton, all of Pickens District.

Issue of February 18, 1829
Married on the 10th instant, by the Rev. Robert Gaines, Mr. Allen Bailey to Miss Sarah, daughter of the Rev. Levi Garrison, both of Anderson District.

Issue of February 25, 1829
Married in Charleston, on the 10th inst., by the Rev. Mr. Gildersleeve, Mr. John B. Ferrell of this place, to Mrs. Jane K. Jenkins, of Charleston.

Issue of March 4, 1829
Married on Thursday evening last, by the Rev. A. W. Ross, Dr. Frederick W. Symmes of this place, to Miss Sarah S., youngest daughter of the last Jos. Whitner, Esq., of this district.

Issue of March 11, 1829
Died on the 5th inst., Martha Jane, only daughter of Mr. Theodore Gaillard, aged 6 years and 10 days.
Died on the 7th February at his residence on Toxaway, Pickens District, Caleb May, Esq., aged 60 years...a native of N. England, but for many years a respectable resident of this state.

Issue of March 18, 1829
Married on Tuesday the 10th inst., by the Rev. S. Vandiver, Mr. James M. Sloan of Pendleton District, to Miss M. A. R. Linton, of Abbeville
Died on the 13th inst., John Franklin, son of Elam Sharpe, aged 4 months.

Issue of March 25, 1829
Died on the ____ instant, Mr. Pendleton Isbell sen. aged about 75 years. He was a native of Virginia and a regular soldier throughout the Revolutionary War, and a strictly honest man

Issue of April 8, 1829
Died on Monday night last, Mr. William Hallum of this district, aged about 45 years.
Died in the Village of Greenville, on Sunday the 29th ult., Mr. Samuel Crayton, merchant of that place.

Died on the 24th ult., at Darlington C. H., while attending to his
official duties, the Hon. Theodore Gaillard, one of the Judges of the
Court of Common Pleas of the State of South Carolina, aged about 62 years.

Issue of May 6, 1829
Married on Thursday last, by the Rev. Levi Garrison, Mr. John Dalton
to Miss Mary, daughter of Charles Hunt, both of Pickens District.

Issue of June 3, 1829
Married on the 26th ult., by the Rev. A. W. Ross, Mr. William Sloan,
of Florida, to Miss Eliza T. Hackett, daughter of Mr. Robert Hackett, of
Franklin Co., Ga.

Issue of June 10, 1829
Married on the 27th ult., by the Rev. Mr. Converse, the Hon. George
M'Duffie to Miss Mary Singleton, daughter of Richard Singleton, Esq., of
Sumpter District.

Issue of June 24, 1829
Married in Tallahassee, Fla., on the 7th inst., by the Rev. Alex. Eck-
man, Mr. Richard B. Bull to Miss Dalcida Lambert, all of that city.

Issue of July 22, 1829
Died in Greensborough, Alabama, on the 17th June, Dr. John Hunter,
formerly for many years, a resident of this place.

Issue of September 2, 1829
Died at his residence near this place, on Monday the 3d inst., of
Bilious Cholic, Mr. Richard H. Harrison, in the 44th year of his age....
a native of S. C., and emigrated to Alabama, among the first settlers
of the county of Tuskalossa, and then removed to the place where we knew
him last...left a wife and 10 orphans, seven of which are females.
Greensboro' (Alab.) Spectator of the 12th ult.

Issue of September 9, 1829
Married at Cornish, NewHampshire, on the 18th ult., by the Rev. Joseph
W. Clary, Rev. Aaron Foster of Pendleton, S. C. to Miss Dorothy Leavitt
of Cornish. They will leave for his residence in Pendleton about 1 Sept.
Married on Tuesday the 1st inst., by the Rev. Mr. Dupre, Mr. John
Gourley to Miss Elizabeth Prince, all of Pickens District.
Died in Columbia, on the 25th ult., Thomas F. Taylor, second son of
Maj. Thomas Taylor jun. of that place...member of the jr. class of S. C.
College.
Died on the 28th ult., at Charlotte, N. C. Jos. Wilson, Esq., an emi-
nent lawyer.
Died on the 23d at Baltimore, John Davidge, M. D., Prof. of anatomy
at the University of Maryland.

Issue of September 16, 1829
Died at his residence in Anderson District, at six o'clock on Tuesday,
the 8th inst., Rev. Moses Holland, in the 71st year of his age and the
47th or 48th year of his ministry. He was interred at the Baptists'
burying ground at Big Creek Church. Rev. Sanford Vandiver delivered a
discourse.

Issue of October 7, 1829
Died on Friday morning, the 25th September, at the residence of Ira
Griffin, Esq, in Abbeville District, Mary Susan, youngest daughter of
Ira and Susan Griffin, aged 10 months and 18 days.

Issue of October 14, 1829
Married at the Cowpens, Walton Co., Ga., the summer residence of Hines
Holt., Esq., on the 22d ult., by the Rev. Mr. Sanford, Nathan L. Hutchins,
Esq., of Lawrenceville, Geo., to Miss Mary D. Holt.
Died in Henry Co., Ga., on the 22d ult., Mrs. Eliza Spencer, wife of
Amasa Spencer, and daughter of the late Thomas Crayton, Esq., of Augusta,
aged 25 years.

Issue of October 21, 1829
Married in Camden on the 8th inst., by the Rev. Mr. Davis, Mr. Ebenezer

P. Niles, to Miss Esther Ann Clarkson, daughter of the late Wm. Clarkson, Jr., Esq.

Married at Sullivan in Ohio, by the Rev. Mr. Child, Richard Lyon, Esq., to Miss Aravesta Lamb.

Issue of October 28, 1829

Married on Thursday evening last, by the Rev. Mr. Ross, Matthew T. Miller to Miss Lucinda, second daughter of Mr. Andrew Harris, all of Pickens District.

Married on Tuesday the 20th inst., by the Rev. S. Vandiver, Mr. John Gambrell to Miss Margaretta Wilson, both of Anderson District.

Died on Saturday morning last, General John M'Million, aged about 65 years. He was an old and well-known inhabitant of this district, having been some years since a member of the House of Representatives of this State, Sheriff of this District and Brig. Gen. of the 1st Brigade.

Died on Monday, the 19th inst., at Alberton, Ga., Mr. Cyrus A. Stuart, aged about 22, a native of this district.

Died on Thursday last at the plantation of Jas. C. Griffin, Doctor Tom, a negro quack...aged 80 or 90 years.

Issue of November 4, 1829

Married on Tuesday the 27th ult., by the Rev. B. D. DuPre, Mr. George H. Taylor to Miss Artimissa, eldest daughter of Col. Jeptha Norton, all of Pickens District.

Issue of November 11, 1829

Married on Tuesday the 3d inst., by William L. Keith, Esq., Mr. James Miller to Miss Rebecca Burch, all of Pickens District.

Issue of November 25, 1829

Died on Friday last at the residence of Mr. Samuel Earle, in Pickens District, Mr. James H. Earle of Greenville, aged about 30 years.

Died about 1st of October last, near Aspalaga, East Florida, Col. John C. Elliott, late of this district, in the 30th year of his age.

Issue of December 2, 1829

Married on Thursday last, by the Rev. Mr. Ozier, Mr. Allen Harbin of Anderson, to Miss Lucinda Gassaway of Pickens District.

Issue of December 16, 1829

Married on the 6th inst., by the Rev. Mr. Ozier, Mr. Francis Reese to Miss Matilda Power, both of Anderson.

Married on Tuesday the 8th inst., by Rev. Wm. Magee, Mr. Samuel Brown to Miss Helena Vandiver, daughter of Rev. Sanford Vandiver.

Married on the 9th inst., by Stephen Williams, Esq., Mr. Robert Jinkins to Miss Lydia Harbor, all of Anderson.

Issue of January 13, 1830

Married on the 22d ult., by the Rev. S. Vandiver, Mr. Isham Sherror to Miss Judith M'Farland, both of Anderson District.

Married on the 29th ult., by the Rev. Robert King, Mr. William Major to Miss Nancy Gambrell, both of Anderson District.

Married on the 29th ult., by James Thompson, Esq., Mr. William Fowler to Miss Elizabeth Haney, both of Anderson District.

Issue of January 20, 1830

Married on the 14th inst., by the Rev. David Humphreys, Mr. Miles Hardy to Miss Eliza, eldest daughter of John Speer, Esq., of Abbeville Dist.

Issue of January 27, 1830

Married at Andersonville, yesterday evening, by the Rev. Mr. Ross, Gen. Joseph N. Whitner to Miss Elizabeth H., only daughter of Mr. James Harrison.

Issue of February 10, 1830

Departed this life on Saturday the 30th ult., in the 55th year of her age, Mrs. Eliza B. Thompson, wife of Judge Thompson, of Greenville Dist.

Died at his residence in Abbeville District, on Thursday night last, Mr. Ira Griffin, aged about 50 years.

Issue of February 17, 1830
Married in Pickens district, on Tuesday the 9th inst., by Rev. George Vandiver, Mr. Leonard Towers, to Miss Sarah, daughter of Maj. David Humphreys.

Issue of February 24, 1830
Married on Thursday last, by James Osborn, Esq., Mr. Alexander M'Kinny to Miss Mary, eldest daughter of Mrs. Mary Barr, both of Anderson District.

Issue of March 3, 1830
Married on Tuesday 23d ult., by Rev. Wm. Magee, Mr. John Griffin to Miss Dorcas daughter of Mr. James M'Coy, all of Anderson District.
Married on Thursday last by Rev. A. Foster, Mr. Robert Lemon to Miss Eliza Cox, all of Anderson District.

Issue of March 24, 1830
Married on Tuesday the 16th inst., by Rev. Mr. Ross, Mr. Andrew Norris to Miss Isabella Robinson.
Married on Thursday last by the Rev. ____, Mr. Charles Winter, to Miss Jane Linn.

Issue of April 14, 1830
Married on the 6th inst., by W. F. Clinkscales, Esq., Mr. Hiram Rivet of North Carolina, to Miss Rhoda, daughter of John Poor, of this district.
Died in the Village of Greenville, on 1st inst., Mrs. Caroline Wickliffe, consort of Capt. William E. Wickliffe, in the 28th year of her age, leaving four children. Mountaineer.
Died on the 7th March, Mrs. Eleanor M. Kirk, of St. John's Berkeley, Charleston District, leaving a son and two daughters.

Issue of May 5, 1830
Married in Charleston on the 20th ult., by Rev. Dr. Palmer, Mr. Thomas J. Pickens of this District, to Miss Kezia A. Miles, of that city.

Issue of May 12, 1830
Married at Decatur, Geo., on the 23d ult., Hezekiah R. Foote, Esq., Attorney at Law to Miss Julia Ann Adams (but a little over ten years old), daughter of John Adams, decd, late merchant of that place.

Issue of May 26, 1830
Died on the 22d inst., at his residence on Seneca River, Mr. Horatio Reese, in the 45th year of his age...a member of the Presbyterian Church.

Issue of June 9, 1830
Died on the 24th ult., Stephen Chastain, Senior, in the 68th year of his age...a native of Virginia, but an inhabitant of this district 42 years ...left widow and several children.

Issue of June 23, 1830
Died on the 4th inst., the Hon. William D. James, a revolutionary officer and lately a Judge of the Court of Common Pleas in this State.
Died at Greensboro' Alabama, on the 22d ult., Mrs. Nancy Hillhouse, wife of Rev. James Hillhouse, formerly of this district.

Issue of June 30, 1830
Married on Thursday last by Rev. George Vandiver, Mr. James B. Clanahan to Miss Sarah Owen of Pickens District.
Died on the 23d Ju , Col. John G. Hunter, aged 26, a native of Pendleton village...left a widowed mother and an only sister.

Issue of July 21, 1830
Married on Tuesday, the 29th ult., by Rev. S. Vandiver, Mr. John H. May of Pickens district to Miss Catherine Pace of Putnam Co., Ga.
Departed this life on the 10th inst., Matthew Dickson, in the 99th year of his age. The deceased was a native of Ireland, emigrated to America in 1752 and was 60 years a resident of this state...a revolutionary soldier...(long eulogy).

34

Issue of August 11, 1830
    Died on Sunday morning, the 25th ult near this place, the Rev. Henry
Gains, in the 94th year of his age. He was born in King & Queen Co., Va.,
and removed to this state when about 60 years old. He resided a few years
in Newberry and Abbeville, and for about 20 years, a resident of this
nieghboorhood...member of the Methodist Church and 50 years a preacher.
He was married three times. His first wife, the mother of his children,
lived to see them all married. The last two he married in old age, but
survived them both.

Issue of September 29, 1830
    Died at the residence of her father, near Manchester, on the 14th
inst., Mrs. Mary Rebecca M'Duffie, consort of Hon. George M'Duffie, and
daughter of Richard Singleton, Esq.

Issue of October 13, 1830
    Married on Thursday last, the 7th inst., by the Rev. S. Vandiver, Mr.
Charles W. Davis to Miss Lucinda Barnett, all of this district.

Issue of October 27, 1830
    Died at Jefferson Barracks, Missouri, on the 20th ult., Lt. James
H. Wright, a native of this state, and graduate of the Military Academy
of 1829.

Issue of November 3, 1830
    Married yesterday evening by Rob't M'Cann, Esq., Mr. Robert Wilson to
Miss Cynthia M'Murry, all of this district.
    Died on Friday last, Mr. Thomas Patterson, an old inhabitant of this
district.

Issue of November 10, 1830
    Married on the 26th October by Rev. William Carlile, Mr. John Erskine,
to Miss Margaret M. Hillhouse, both of this district.
    Died on Thursday evening, the 4th inst., at the residence of John
Thompson, Esq., Dr. William Calhoun Norris, aged 34 years and 10 months...
left a widow and four small children.

Issue of November 17, 1830
    Married on Thursday last by William L. Keith, Esq., Mr. Bartley W. F.
Capehart to Miss Polly Blackburn, all of Pickens.

Issue of November 24, 1830
    Married on Thursday, the 18th inst., by ____, Col. David McKinney, of
Pickens District, to Miss Nancy, daughter of ____ Tal'y, Esq., of Greenville District.

Issue of January 5, 1831
    Married on Thursday, the 24th ult., by John Myers, Esq., Mr. Samuel
Johnson to Miss Mary M'Kinley, all of Pickens District.
    Married on the same day, by William Swords, Esq., Mr. James Whitten
to Miss Jane, daughter of Benjamin Smith of Anderson District.

Issue of January 26, 1831
    Married on Thursday last by Rev. Aaron Foster, Mr. George W. Knox of
Pickens District, to Miss Maria, daughter of H. D. Reese, Esq., of this
district.
    Married on the same day by Joseph Grisham, Esq., Mr. W. D. C. Daniel
to Miss Frances, daughter of Mr. James Grant, all of Pickens district.
    Died in Anderson District, on the 10th inst., Mrs. Jane, wife of
Robert M'Cann, Esq., in the 67th year of her age...for many years a member
of the Church of Christ.

Issue of February 2, 1831
    Married on Thursday last by the Rev. A. W. Ross, Mr. James Hammett to
Miss Polly M'Dow, both of Pickens District.
    Married on the 26th ult., by the Rev. Mr. Carlile, Mr. Benjamin Heaton
to Miss Lydia, daughter of Mr. Salathiel Heaton, all of Anderson District.
    Married on the 27th, by the same, Mr. Luke Hamilton to Miss Rosannah,
daughter of Mr. Lemuel Hall.

Issue of February 16, 1831
Married on Thursday, the 3d inst., by the Rev. W. Carlile, Mr. Hugh D.
Law to Miss Nancy Erskine.
Married on the 20th ult., by Rev. David Humphreys, Mr. James W. Weems,
to Miss Jane Speer, both of Abbeville District.
Died on the 6th inst., in Spartanburg District, Mrs. Anna A. Moore,
wife of Dr. A. B. Moore, of that District...(eulogy).

Issue of March 2, 1831
Married on the 17th ult., by the Right Rev. Bishop Bowen, Mr. Benjamin
Huger, eldest son of Col. F. K. Huger to Miss Celestine, daughter of Col.
Thomas Pinckney.
Married on the same day, by Rev. David Humphreys, Col. William H.
Caldwell to Mrs. Ellington, both of Abbeville District.

Issue of March 9, 1831
Married on Tuesday evening, the 22d ult., by Rev. Sanford Vandiver,
Mr. Thomas Burrough to Miss Matilda Warnock, both of Anderson District.
Married on the 27th by the same, Mr. John Thomas, to Miss Sarah Addis,
of Pickens.
Died on the 28th ult., in Pickens District, John Halbert Sitton, son
of John Sitton, Jr., aged 9 months and 14 days...the youngest and only
brother to seven sisters.

Issue of March 23, 1831
Married on the 18th inst., by Joseph Grisham, Esq., of this place, Mr.
Francis Bradley, in the 80th year of his age, to Mrs. Polly Eubanks, about
40 years of age, both of Pickens District.

Issue of April 6, 1831
Married on the 17th ult., by Rev. Sandford Vandiver, Mr. Charles P.
Dean to Miss Lucinda Horton, both of Anderson.
Married on the 22d ult., by the same, Mr. John Edmondson to Miss Polly
Farmer.
Married on the 24th ult., by the Rev. Levi Garrison, Mr. Elisha Smith
to Miss Elizabeth Dilashey, all of Anderson.
Died at his residence in Coweta Co., Ga., on the 10th of March, Col.
John Dickson, aged 63. He was long a resident of this District, and left
a wife and a large family of children.

Issue of April 20, 1831
Married on the 14th inst., by Rev. S. Vandiver, Mr. John W. Overby to
Miss Elizabeth, daughter of Robert Wilson, both of Anderson Village.
Married in Beaufort, on the evening of the 6th inst., by Rev. Joseph
T. Walker, Dr. Arthur S. Gibbs, of Pendleton, to Miss Phoebe S. Campbell,
of that place.
Died at his residence in this vicinity, on the 14th inst., Zachariah
Taliaferro, aged 72 years, by birth a Virginia, but adopted Carolina, a
citizen of Pendleton, one of the first in this settlement...a revolutionary
soldier...(long eulogy).

Issue of April 27, 1831
Married on yesterday evening by Rev. Rodolphus Dickinson, Francis
Burt Jur., Esq., to Miss George Ann Hall.
Married on the 21st ult., by Rev. S. Vandiver, Mr. Robert White to
Miss Mary W. Cobb, both of Anderson District.
Died on Monday the 1st inst., Mr. Andrew W. M'Dow, aged 23 years.

Issue of May 25, 1831
Married in Rutherford, N. C., on the 10th inst., by Rev. John Gibbs,
the Hon. Samuel P. Carson to Miss S. Catharine Wilson, daughter of James
Wilson, Esq., of Tennessee.
Married in Tennessee, Mr. Benjamin McCary to Miss Eunice Cogswell.
Married in Camden on the 12th inst., Thomas J. Wethers, Esq., to Miss
Elizabeth Roykin.
Married in Columbia, on the 19th , Maj. James O'Hanlon, to Miss Eliza-
beth, daughter of Col. D. Myers.
Died on the 15th inst., at Hamburg, S. C., Mrs. Artimissa Taylor, wife
of George H. Taylor, eldest daughter of Col. Jeptha Norton of Pickens
District. She was 24 years of age, had been married about 18 months...
left a husband and young child.

Issue of June 15, 1831
    Married in the village of Anderson, on Thursday evening last, by the
Rev. Richard B. Cater, Mr. Van A. Lawhon, to Miss Lucretia, daughter of
Mr. John Archer.

Issue of June 22, 1831
    Married on Tuesday the 14th inst., by Jas. Gaines, Esq., Mr. Samuel B.
Judon, to Miss Ruth daughter of Capt. William M'Dow, all of Pickens Dist.
    Married on the 9th inst., John T. Carter, Esq. of Clarkesville, Ga.,
to Miss Eliza Daniel of Spartanburg District, S. C.
    Died on Saturday evening last, Augustus Ludlow, only son of Wm. Steele,
aged 2 years and 9 months.

Issue of June 29, 1831
    Died on Friday the 17th inst., Robert M'Cann, Esq., aged about 68
years. He was a native of Ireland, but emigrated to this country in his
youth.

Issue of July 27, 1831
    Married on Sunday evening last, by Stephen Williams, Esq., Mr. Thomas
J. Hughes, to Mrs. Lucinda Oliver, all of Anderson Village.

Issue of August 10, 1831
    Died on Thursday last, at Greenville, John H. Goodlett, Esq., Clerk of
Court for that District, aged about 42 years.

Issue of August 24, 1831
    Married on Thursday evening last, by Rev. D. Derrick, Mr. Jeremiah
Winter, to Miss Hannah L., eldest daughter of Mr. William K. Hamilton, all
of this District.
    Married on the same evening, by William Swords, Esq., Mr. Elijah Whit-
ten to Miss Jane Mulligan.

Issue of August 31, 1831
    Married on the 21st inst., by Rev. Sanford Vandiver, Mr. Asa Clink-
scales, to Miss Nancy Kay, both of Anderson District.

Issue of September 7, 1831
    Married on Wednesday evening, the 24th ultimo, by Rev. Aaron Foster,
Mr. Peter A. Bertrand of this place, to Miss Susan, daughter of Capt.
Crosby W. Miller, of Pickens District.

Issue of September 14, 1831
    Married yesterday evening, in the Presbyterian Church, by Rev. Aaron
Foster, Mr. William J. Kanuff to Miss Serena C. Bailey, both of this place.

Issue of September 21, 1831
    Married on the 13th inst., by Rev. D. Humphreys, Mr. S. Shackleford
of Abbeville to Miss Melissa, daughter of Maj. Lewis of Anderson District.

Issue of October 12, 1831
    Died at the residence of her father, in Greenville District, in the
27th year of her age, Mrs. Louisa M. Manigault, wife of Peter Manigault,
Esq., of Charleston. (eulogy).

Issue of October 26, 1831
    Married on the 23d, by J. T. Lewis Esq., Mr. Seth Risener, to Miss
Catherine Ingraham, both of Anderson District.
    Married on the 18th inst., by Joseph Grisham, Esq., Mr. Elijah Garrett
to Miss Elizabeth McDaniel, both of Pickens District.

Issue of November 2, 1831
    Married on Thursday last, by the Rev. Robert Gaines, Mr. William P.
M'Dow to Miss Margaret A. Jaudon, all of Pickens District.
    Married on the same evening, by Rev. A. W. Ross, Mr. Zephaniah Smith
to Miss Anna, eldest daughter of Mr. Joseph Watkins, all of this District.
    Died on Sunday morning, the 23d ult., Col. Richard Lewis, aged about
67...a native of Albemarle Co., Va., but removed in early life to Rutherford, N. C. About 13 years ago, he removed to this neighborhood...leaves
a large family of children.

Died on Wednesday last, at his residence on Deep Creek, at the age of about 90 years, Maj. James Hamilton, a soldier of the Revolution (eulogy).

Issue of November 16, 1831
Died at his residence on Deep Creek, in this District, on the 11th inst., Mr. Charles Webb, aged about 64 years...member of the Baptist Church.

Issue of November 23, 1831
Died at Edgefield C. H., on the 17th inst., Col. Eldred Simkins, sen., formerly a Representative in Congress.
Died in New York, on the 6th inst., Col. James Dunlap, formerly of this State, and recently appointed U. S. Attorney for the Middle District of Florida.

Issue of November 30, 1831
Married on Wednesday evening last, by the Rev. David Derrick, Mr. Hezekiah Newton, to Miss Elizabeth West, all of this district.

Issue of December 14, 1831
Married on the 6th inst., by Rev. S. Vandiver, Mr. Joseph Stevenson to Miss Mary Russell. On the 8th inst., by the same, Mr. Orance Burroughs to Miss Eliza D. Magee, all of Anderson District.
Died on the 4th inst., in Pickens District, Mr. James Hunter, a native of Pennsylvania, but for many years a resident of this place where he died. He was about 56 years of age, left a wife and 9 children.

Issue of December 21, 1831
Married on Tuesday the 13th inst., by Rev. D. Hutchins, Mr. Elias Miller, to Miss Jane Rodgers, all of Anderson District.

Issue of December 28, 1831
Married on the 15th inst., by the Rev. Mr. Ballard, Mr. Simpson Abbett to Miss Narcissa, eldest daughter of Mr. John Adair, all of Pickens Dist.
Married on the 20th inst., by Rev. Mr. Hembree, Mr. William M'Clure to Miss Parry Barnett, all of Anderson District.
Married on the village of Pendleton, on Thursday last, by James C. Girffin, Esq., Mr. Hezekiah Kelly to Miss Vashti Davis.
Married on the same day, by Rev. Wm. Magee, Mr. Bailey Kay to Miss Polly N, daughter of Mr. William Barron.
Married on the same evening, by th same, Mr. J. S. Magee, to Miss Lucinda S. Acker, youngest daughter of the widow Acker, all of Pickens District.
Died on 10 November last, in Madison Co., Ill, within a few miles of St. Louis, Mr. Thomas T. Hunter, son of the late Dr. William Hunter of this district, in the 22d year of his age.

Issue of January 4, 1832
Married on the 25th ult., by Rev. Drury Hutchins, Mr. William Murphey to Miss Elizabeth, daughter of R. Leathers, all of Pickens District.
Married on the same day, by Rev. Levi Garrison, Mr. Joel West, late of Spartanburg, to Miss Anna, daughter of Daniel Hix, of Anderson District.

Issue of January 18, 1832
Married on Thursday last, in Pickens District, by the Rev. Charles Durham, Mr. William Hunter, to Miss Sarah Ann, daughter of Maj. A. Hamilton.
Married on the same evening, by the same, Mr. ___ Sheriff to Miss Polly Mauldin.
Married on the 3d inst., by Rev. David Humphreys, Mr. Jesse Bryan to Miss Martha Parker; also on the 5th inst., Mr. William Henderson to Miss Martha Watts, all of Anderson District.
Married on the 5th inst., by the Rev. Levi Garrison, Mr. Thomas James of Georgia, to Mrs. Amy Smith of Anderson-

Issue of January 25, 1832
Married last evening in this village, by the Rev. Richard B. Cater, Mr. John T. Sloan to Miss Eliza Ann, eldest daughter of Mr. E. B. Benson.

Issue of February 8, 1832
Married on Thursday last, by Rev. A. Foster, Mr. William S. Rowland to Miss Florida, daughter of Mr. H. D. Reese, all of Anderson District.

Issue of February 22, 1832
Married in Pickens District, on Thursday evening last, by Rev. B. D. DuPre, Mr. Zachariah Hall to Miss Ruth Jenkins, daughter of Francis Jenkins, Esq.
Married in Anderson District, on the 9th inst., by Rev. Wm Carlile, Mr. Joel H. Berry to Miss Martha E. Simpson.
Married on the 16th by the same, Mr. John Pratt of Abbeville to Miss Nancy N. Harkness of Anderson.

Issue of February 29, 1832
Married in Pickens district on Thursday, the 23d inst., by William L. Keith, Esq., Mr. James Lewis to Miss Adaline Duff. On Thursday, the 16th inst., by Rev. Mr. Murphy, Mr. Lively to Miss Bolen. On the same day, by William Hunter, Esq., Mr. Joseph Durham to Miss Elizabeth Alexander.

Issue of March 26, 1832
Married on the 1st inst., by Rev. Wm. Murphy, Mr. Joseph Winchester to Miss ___ Miller, daughter of Isaac Miller sen. On the same day, by Bailey Barton, Esq., Mr. John Cantrell to Miss Nancy, daughter of Rev. Charles Durham.

Issue of March 28, 1832
Married on Thursday, the 22d inst., by John T. Lewis, Esq., Mr. James Moore to Miss Lucinda Brown, all of Anderson District.
Married on the same evening by Joseph Cox., Esq., Mr. George Poor to Miss Tempy, daughter of Mr. John Holland, both of Anderson District.

Issue of April 25, 1832
Died in Thursday the 12th inst., Mr. John Brownlow, a soldier of the Revolution, and for many years an honest resident of this district.
Died in Camden on the 16th inst., Col. John Taylor, of Columbia, in the 63d year of his age...Col. T. was formerly Governor of this State.

Issue of May 9, 1832
Married on the 3d inst., by Rev. D. Hutchins, Mr. Elisha Webb to Miss Nancy King, both of Anderson District.

Issue of May 16, 1832
Married on the 25th inst., by Rev. Mr. Ross, Mr. Robert Purvis of Columbia, to Miss Mary, daughter of Gen. John B. Earle of this District.
Married on Thursday last in the village of Greenville, by the Rev. Mr. Gibson, William Choice, Esq., to Miss Caroline M., daughter of Mr. Jeremiah Cleveland.

Issue of May 23, 1832
Died on Wednesday night last, Mrs. Piety Davis, in the 80th year of her age...an inhabitant of this District for 40 years, and a pious member of the Baptist Church...left a very numerous family of children.

Issue of May 30, 1832
Married in Pickens District, on the 15th inst., by Rev. William Murphree, Mr. Alexander Cooper, to Miss Elizabeth Brown.

Issue of June 6, 1832
Married on the 29th ult., by William L. Keith, Esq., Mr. John Hammett to Miss Lucinda Kelly, all of Pickens District.

Issue of June 13, 1832
Gen. Thomas Sumter died on the 1st inst. at Stateburg.

Issue of July 11, 1832
Married last evening by Rev. Mr. Ross, Mr. Robert Anderson, Jr. to Miss Mary B. Pickens.
Died at Greenville, S. C. on the 1st inst., in the 36th year of her age, Mrs. Anna Isabella, wife of Rev. P. H. Folkey, and daughter of the late William Bay.

Issue of July 25, 1832
Died in this village on Monday morning, the 23d inst., Miss Rebecca Whitner, daughter of the late Joseph Whitner, Esq., of this district... (eulogy).

Issue of August 1, 1832
Married on Thursday evening last, by Joshua Fields, Esq., Mr. Hugh Duncan to Miss Jane Wright, both of this district.
Married on the 26th ult., by Rev. B. D. DuPre, Mr. Anderson Jenkins to Miss Phoebe, daughter of Zachariah Hall, all of Pickens District.

Issue of August 15, 1832
Married on Thursday evening last, by the Rev. Dr. Waddell, Mr. James A. Cherry, to Miss Elizabeth, eldest daughter of Mr. Horatio Reese, decd.

Issue of September 5, 1832
Married on Thursday last by Rev. David Derrick, Mr. John Adams to Miss Sarah Winter.
Died on the 27th August last, at his residence in Abbeville District, Mr. William Miller, in the 35th year of his age...left a widowed mother, two brothers and a sister.

Issue of September 12, 1832
Married on Thursday last, by Miles M. Norton, Esq., Mr. John Caminarde to Miss Polly Miller, all of this place.
Married on the 6th inst., by Rev. Robert Gaines, Mr. Robert Copeland to Miss Sarah Neil, all of Pickens District.
Married on the 19th August, by Joseph Cox, Esq., Mr. Smallwood Dalton to Miss Rebecca Erskew, both of Anderson District..
Died on the 8th August 1832, Mr. John Mills in the 67th year of his age...a Native of North Carolina, removed to this State in 1800, an inhabitant of this district ever since.

Issue of October 3, 1832
Died on Thursday, the 20th inst., John T. Lewis, Esq., aged about 45 years...a native of N. C., but an inhabitant of this District, of which he has been Clerk of Court, for more than 20 years...left a widow and several children.
Died on his way from Charleston to Pendleton (of the fever), Mr. W. Eldrich, of the firm of Eldrich and Preston, in the 26th year of his age.

Issue of October 10, 1832
Married on the 27th ult., by the Rev. B. D. DuPre, Mr. William H. Stribling, to Miss Jane M'Kinley, all of Pickens District.

Issue of October 31, 1832
Married on Thursday the 25th inst., by the Rev. Robert King, Mr. Robert C. Duckworth, to Miss Elizabeth, second daughter of the late Hon. John Wilson.
Married on Tuesday evening the 23d inst., by the Rev. W. Magee, Mr. William Townes, to Miss Chloe, daughter of W. F. Clinkscales, Esq.
Also by the same on Thursday evening, the 25th inst., Mr. Joshua Burriss to Miss Rachel Clements, all of Anderson District.

Issue of November 14, 1832
Married on last evening, by J. C. Griffith, Esq., Mr. William J. Gass to Mrs. Sophia Russell, all of this District.
Married on Thursday the 25th ult., by B. Dickson, Esq., Mr. Stephen F. Chastain to Miss Pamelia Hudgins, all of Anderson District.

Issue of November 28, 1832
Charles Carroll of Carrollton, died in the 77th year, on the 14th inst., the sole survivor of the signers of the Declaration of Independence. (Charles Carroll was a signer from Maryland--BHH).
Married on Tuesday evening, the 20th inst., by the Rev. Levi Garrison, Mr. James Foster of Union District, to Miss Nancy White of this district.

Issue of December 5, 1832
Married on last evening at Anderson C. H., by Rev. Sanford Vandiver, Mr. Benson Robert, to Miss Eveline, daughter of Maj. Thomas Benson, of Greenville.

Issue of December 12, 1832
Married on the 27th ult., by the Rev. D. Humphries, Dr. Matthew Lockhart of Abbeville, to Miss Lucinda, youngest daughter of Samuel Cunningham, Esq., of Laurens District.
Married on Wednesday the 28th ult., at the Falls, Pickens Dist., by Rev. Stephen Ellis, Thomas Watson, Esq., to Miss Melinda C., daughter of John Grisham sen., Esq., all of that district.
Died on Saturday morning, the 8th inst., in the 50th year of his age, Mr. Robert Hackett, a citizen of Anderson District, and an orderly member of the Methodist Episcopal Church at Ebenezer. At an early period in life, Mr. Hackett's parens emigrated from the State of Virginia, Richmond Co., to S. C., Abbeville District. They settled near Cambridge, and he, for the health of his family, removed to Anderson District in January 1829.
Died on the 25th inst., in Habersham Co., Ga., Mrs. Anna, consort of William Thompson, Jr...left a husband and five small children.

Issue of December 26, 1832
Married on Thursday evening, by the Rev. D. Derrick, Mr. Jefferson Hallum to Miss Catherine Kirksey, all of Pickens District.
Married on Thursday, the 20th inst., by Rev. William Magee, Mr. Thomas Geer to Miss Sarah, daughter of Mr. Levi Clinkscales.
Married on Thursday, the 20th inst., by Rev. Mr. DuPre, Mr. Geo. Verner to Miss Harriet, daughter of Mr. Richard Harris, all of Pickens District.

Issue of January 2, 1833
Married on the 13th ult., by Rev. D. Humphreys, Maj. Wm Dickson of Anderson District, to Miss Marian Anderson, of Abbeville District.
Married at candle light on the same day, by the same, Mr. Wm Spear to Miss Jane Norwood, both of Abbeville.

Issue of January 9, 1833
Married on Tuesday the 1st inst., by Rev. R. D. DuPre, Mr. Joseph Donaldson, to Mrs. Melinda Cannon, daughter of Mr. Jeremiah Fields, all of Pickens District.
Married on the same day, by Rev. Stephen Ellis, Mr. Martin Moss to Miss Rebecca Cox, of the same district.
Married on Tuesday evening, the 18th ult., by Rev. S. Vandiver, Mr. Joel S. Gambrell to Miss Jane Williams, all of Anderson District.

Issue of January 23, 1833
Married on Wednesday evening, the 16th inst. by Rev. Mr. Cater, Mr. Joseph P. Harris of this District, to Miss Ann T., second daughter of Col. R. Anderson, of Pickens District.
Married on Thursday the 17th inst., by Rev. Wm. Magee, Mr. John Clinkscales to Miss Eliza Ann Wrainch, daughter of Capt. Robert B. Norris.

Issue of January 30, 1833
Married on Thursday evening last, by Rev. Dr. Bat, Mr. Samuel Reid of Pickens, to Miss Caroline, daughter of James Thomson, of Anderson District.
Married on Tuesday, the 22d inst., by Rev. Sanford Vandiver, Mr. Henry Holmes(?) to Miss Telitha A. McGee(?) of Anderson District.

Issue of February 6, 1833
Married on the 31st ult., by Rev. D. Hutchins, Mr. Samuel P. Cobb to Miss Margaret Malissa, daughter of James Griffin, Esq., all of this dist.

Issue of February 13, 1833
Married on Thursday evening, by Rev. Mr. Carlile, Mr. Mauldin R. Manning to Miss Sabina McPhail, both of this district.

Issue of February 20, 1833
Married on the 3d inst., by William Berry, Esq., Mr. William Kelly, aged 74 years to Miss Lucinda Harris, aged 17 years, both of Elbert Co., Ga.

Issue of February 27, 1833
Departed this life on Friday morning, the 22d inst., in the 75th year of his age, Mr. Nathaniel Duncan, a zealous member of the Methodist Church.
Married on Thursday last by the Rev. Mr. Cater, Mr. Richard T. Wilson to Miss Martha, youngest daughter of John Miller, Esq., decd, both of this place.

Married on Thursday, the 14th inst., by Rev. Mr. Anthony, Mr. William Robinson to Miss Mary Ann Wilson, both of this District.

Issue of March 6, 1833
Married on the 28th ult., by Rev. Mr. Magee, Mr. Richmond T. Rutledge to Miss Caroline C., daughter of Capt. Robert B. Norris.

Issue of March 20, 1833
Married on Sunday evening, the 10th inst., by E. S. Norris, Esq., Mr. William Tete to Miss Patsey Howard.

Issue of April 17, 1833
Died at his residence in Pickens District, on the 30th ult., Elihu Creswell, formerly of Abbeville, but for many years a high respected citizen of our district.

Issue of April 24, 1833
Departed this life on the 7th inst., at his residence in this district, Andrew Liddell, sen., aged about 83 years...born in Newcastle Co., Md., where he resided until he was nearly grown. He settled in Abbeville Dist., where he continued during the Revolutionary War. Two of his brothers were killed. In 1790, he settled in Pendleton District, at the place on which he died...left 6 sons, 3 daughters, 72 grandchildren, and 35 great-grand-children...member of the Presbyterian Church...(eulogy).

Issue of May 1, 1833
Married on the 18th ult., by Rev. D. Humphries, Mr. Donald Ferguson of Monroe Co., Ga., to Miss Jane Beaty of this District.

Issue of May 15, 1833
Married yesterday evening, by the Rev. Richard B. Cater, Mr. George W. Bomar of Anderson Village, to Miss Emily C., daughter of Capt. D. Sloan, of Pickens District.

Issue of June 19, 1833
Departed this life on the 12th May, Anderson District, Mr. Andrew Young, aged about 80 years. During the Revolution, Mr. Young was in several engagements with the British, the Indians, and the Tories...a ruling elder in the Presbyterian Church.
Died on Monday, the 18th inst., Amanda, daughter of John F. Maw, aged 2 years, 11 months and 10 days.

Issue of July 17, 1833
Departed this life on Saturday, the 12th inst., Rebecca Ann, youngest daughter of Rev. Richard B. Cater, aged 1 year, 1 month, 20 days.

Issue of July 24, 1833
Died a few weeks since in Pickens District, Rev. George Vandiver, a soldier of the Revolution and clergyman of the Baptist persuasion.

Issue of July 31, 1833
Married on the 9th inst., at "Dolche Sperande," Greenville District, S. C., by Rev. Mr. Ross, William Brooks, Esq., of Mobile, Ala., to Catherine Rose, daughter of Dr. Ioor, of said district.

Issue of August 7, 1833
Departed this life on the 16th ult., William Henry, only child of Mr. William J. Knaufe of our Village, aged 9 months and 8 days.

Issue of August 14, 1833
Married on the 1st inst., by Rev. David Humphreys, Mr. John Wakefield of Abbeville to Miss Mary Buchanan of Anderson District.

Issue of September 11, 1833
Died on the 12 August near Pickens C. H., Mr. Thomas Blackburn, a young man of excellent character.
Died on the 1st inst., at the residence of W. Carter, Esq., near this place, Mr. Thomas Ogier, a well-known citizen of Charleston, aged 79 years.

Issue of September 18, 1833
Departed this life after an illness of seven days only, on Friday evening the 13th inst., Capt. James Thomson, in the 64th year of his age. He was one of the first settlers in this District, in the Rocky River neighborhood...for many years an elder in the Presbyterian Church. In 1812, during the late war, he was elected to the command of a company, in which he headed an expedition to the Creek Nation.

Issue of September 25, 1833
Died about 4 o'clock yesterday morning, at the residence of Col. John E. Calhoun, Mr. John Schulz of Charleston.

Died on Thursday morning last, Edward Ogier, aged about 16 years, son of the Late Mr. Thomas Ogier of Charleston, whose death was announced a few weeks since...was accidentally shot.

Issue of October 2, 1833
Died on Monday, 30th September, Mr. Elisha Bennett, Sen., in the 67th year of his age...resided on the plantation where he died 40 or 50 years.

Issue of October 9, 1833
Married on Tuesday evening, the 1st inst., by the Rev. Levi Garrison, Jas. Palmer to Miss Darkes Looney, both of Anderson District.

Married on the 3d inst., by W. M'Murry, Esq., Mr. George Wigginton to Miss Mary, daughter of Mrs. West, all of Anderson District.

Issue of October 30, 1833
Married on Tuesday the 22d instant, by the Rev. Mr. Barnwell, William Van Wyck, Esq., of the city of New York, to Miss Lydia An Maverick, of this district.

Married on the 22d inst., by Rev. Richard B. Cater, Major Thomas H. M'Cann, to Miss Narcissa, daughter of Mr. Wm. Walker of Pickens District.

Married on the 17th inst., by William L., Keith, Esq., Mr. Thomas R. Brackenridge to Miss Laura, daughter of Mr. Elisha Lawrence of Pickens.

Married in Princeton, N. J. on the 1st inst., by Rev. Dr. Miller, the Rev. W. C. M'Elroy of Pendleton, S. C. to Miss Harriet T.,daughter of the late John N. Simpson, Esq., of the former place.

Married on the 25th inst., by Rev. Levi Garrison, Mr. Gillam Shearer to Miss Casey R. Rodgers, all of Anderson District.

Married on the 6th inst., by the Rev. Mr. M'Call, Mr. William Brown to Miss Serena Shearer, both of Anderson District.

Married on the 17th inst., by Esq. Moorhead, Mr. John Hays, to Miss Elizabeth Smith, all of Anderson District.

Issue of November 6, 1833
Married on Thursday evening, the 10th inst., by the Rev. Wm. Magee, Mr. Oliver M. Bigbee of Abbeville District, to Miss Mary Clements, daughter of Capt. Hugh Clements of Anderson District.

Married on the 24th ult., by A. J. Liddell, Esq., Mr. James Kimbrell to Miss Rebecca, daughter of Samson Barnet, all of Anderson District.

Issue of November 13, 1833
Married on the 31st October last, by the Rev. S. Vandiver, Mr. James M. Bell of Abbeville to Miss Nancy Hall, of this district.

Married on the 31st ult., by Rev. Mr. M'Call, Mr. James M. Henderson of Elbert Co., Ga., to Miss Elizabeth A., only daughter of Mr. Westley Earp of Anderson.

Married on the 7th inst., by Squire Moorhead, Mr. James M'Losky to Miss Elizabeth Duncan, both of this District.

Issue of November 20, 1833
Married on Tuesday the 13th inst., by William L. Keith, Esq., Mr. Christopher Kirksey to Miss Sarah Sutherland, all of Pickens District.

Married on the 14th inst., by Rev. David Humphreys, Mr. Buckner G. Christopher to Miss Sarah Cozby, both of Abbeville District.

Married on the 7th by the same, Mr. Elijah Elrod to Miss Thyrsa Skelton, both of this District.

Departed this life on the 10th inst., at the residence of Samuel J. Hammond, Mrs. Lucy Hammond, in the 84th year of her age...member of the Methodist Church.

43

Issue of November 27, 1833
    Married on Monday the 18th inst., by Wm. Hunter, Esq., Mr. Henry
Meriam to Miss Elenor Smith, all of Pickens District.
    Died very suddenly, at his residence in Pickens District, on Saturday
morning last, Mr. Samuel Earle, aged 73 years...he was actively engaged
in the Revolution, and was many years ago, a representative in Congress.
    Death of Hon. William D. Martin, Judge of the South Eastern Circuit.
Charleston Mercury, 18th inst.
    Death of Col. Thomas Taylor. Col. Thomas Taylor died on Sunday morn-
ing, at the residence of his son, Mr. Benjamin Taylor. He was born in
Amelia Co., Va 10 Sept 1743. Columbia Telescope, 19th inst.

Issue of December 4, 1833
    Married on the 26th ult., by Rev. S. Vandiver, Mr. Larkin Vandiver to
Miss Sarah, daughter of Mr. William Williams, both of Anderson District.
    Death of Maj. James Hamilton, father of Gen. Hamilton...died on the
night of the 25th inst., in the 83 year of his age. He was the oldest
surviving field officer of the regular line of the Continental army.
Char Mercury

Issue of December 11, 1833
    Married on the 5th inst., by Rev. D. Humphreys, Mr. Thomas Skelton to
Miss Eliza Martin, both of this District.

Issue of December 18, 1833
    Married yesterday evening by the Rev. Benj. D. Dupre, Mr. Benjamin
Hawes, to Miss Anna M., daughter of Mr. William Hallen, deceased.
    Married in this village on Thursday, the 5th inst., by the Rev. Stephen
Ellis, Mr. Elijah Alexander Jr. to Miss Elizabeth Steele.

Issue of December 25, 1833
    Married on the 5th inst., by JamesGriffin, Esq., Miss Mary O'Barr of
Anderson District to Mr. Hamilton Frazier of Gwinnett Co., Geo.
    Married on the 10th inst., by Rev. Levi Garrison, Miss Sarah Rochester
of Anderson District, to Mr. William Smith of Pickens District.
    Married on the 12th inst., by the Rev. R. Gaines, Mr. Zachariah Powers
to Miss Nancy Arnold, all of Pickens District.
    Married on Thursday the 12th inst., by the Rev. Samuel More, Mr.
William Crocker of Georgia, to Miss Mary Hix of Anderson.
    Married on the 13th by the Rev. Levi Garrison, Mr. George Newell to
Miss Jane Herron, both of Anderson.
    Married on the 19th inst., by Rev. David Humphreys, Mr. Joel Dunn of
Elbert Co., Ga., to Mis Ann Turner of this District.
    Died at Mount St. Mary's College, on the first ultimo, John L. Ogier,
aged 14 years and 7 months.

Issue of January 1, 1834
    Married on Tuesday evening, the 17th ult., by the Rev. William Magee,
Mr. William M. Alexander to Miss Martha M'Daniel, both of Greenville Dist.
    Married on the 19th by the same, Mr. William Enochs, to Miss Elizabeth
Snyder, both of Greenville Village.
    Married on the 20th by Alex. Moorhead, Esq., Mr. Ezekiel George to
Miss Elizabeth, daughter of Mr. Manning Pool,both of this District.
    Married on the 19th by Rev. S. Vandiver, Mr. George Roberts to Miss
Catherine, daughter of Francis Burt Sen., Esq.,
    Died on Saturday morning last, near this place, aged about 50 years,
Mr. John Adams...left a widow and several children.

Issue of January 8, 1834
    Died on Tuesday, the 17th December last, Mrs. Martha E. Berry, late
consort of Joel H. Berry, and daughter of Archibald Simpson of this
District. She had just entered her 21st year, and had been married a few
days over 1 year and 10 months...member of ths Presbyterian Church.

Issue of January 15, 1834
    Married on 24 December last, by Rev. D. Humphreys, Mr. James M'Lees
to Miss Eleanor Searight, of Anderson District.
    Married on the 2d of January, by the same, Mr. John M'Bride, to Miss
Pamelia Morrow of Abbeville.
    Married on the 31st December, by Rev. William Magee, Mr. Samuel A.

Magee of Anderson District, to Miss Nancy, daughter of Mr. Humphrey Cobb, of Greenville District.

Issue of January 22, 1834
Married on the 16th inst., by Rev. Levi Garrison, Mr. Almon Hutchins to Miss Margaret Adeline, daughter of Mr. Geo. Swilling, of Anderson Dist.

Issue of February 5, 1834
Married on the 23d ult., in the village of Pickens by the Rev. Mr. Ross, Samuel A. Townes, Esq., of Abbeville to Miss Joanna L., youngest daughter of the late Dr. George Hall, formerly of Charleston.
Married on the 28th ult., by Rev. Robert Gaines, Mr. Simpson Hagood to Miss Elizabeth, daughter of Rev. Levi Garrison, of Anderson District.
Married on the 9th ult., by the Rev. David Humphreys, Mr. John M'Lin to Miss Elizabeth A. Simpson.
Married on the 21st by the same, Mr. James Kennedy to Miss Jane Wasson, all of this district.
Married on the 23d by the same, Mr. John White to Miss Sarah M'Allister both of Abbeville District.

Issue of February 12, 1834
Married on Thursday, the 30th January, by Rev. D. Humphreys, Mr. Alexander Gilliland, to Miss _____ Skelton, both of this District.
Married on Thursday last, by Rev. R. B. Cater, Mr. John F. Miller to Miss Catherine Crawford, of Anderson.
Married in Pickens District, on the 6th inst., Mr. Carter Clayton to Miss Sarah, daughter of Mr. James Hunter, decd.

Issue of February 19, 1834
Married on 30th January last, by A. J. Liddell, Esq., Mr. Eli Clark to Miss Pamelia Thomas, all of Anderson District.
Died in the village of Anderson, on Saturday morning, the 15th inst., at 2 o'clock, Mrs. Eliza T. McCully, wife of Stephen McCully, and daughter of Archibald McElroy...left an infant not quite three months old... member of the Presbyterian Church...(eulogy). The funeral sermon was announced to be at Sandy Spring Meeting House by Rev. Mr. Ross.

Issue of February 26, 1834
Married in Pickens District, on Wednesday evening last, by Rev. T. Dawson, James B. Mays, Esq., of Florida, to Miss Damaris Miriam, daughter of the late Samuel Earle, Esq.

Issue of March 19, 1834
Married on the 6th inst., in Pickens District, by _____, Mr. Elias Earle to Miss Harriet, daughter of the late Samuel Earle, Esq.
Married on the 23d February, by the Rev. David Humphreys, Mr. Alexander Oliver to Miss Louisa Hogg, both of Abbeville.
Married on the 27th by the Rev. D. Humphreys, Mr. John Early to Miss Mary McPhitridge, of this District.

Issue of March 26, 1834
Married on Thursday evening last, by the Rev. Robert Gaines, Mr. Lemuel G. Hamilton, to Miss Clemelia, only daughter of Mr. John Arial, all of Pickens District.
Died recently in this district, Mr. William Noble, aged 90, a Revolutionary soldier.

Issue of April 9, 1834
Married on the 1st inst., by Rev. Whitefield Anthony, Mr. Peyton Holliman of Abbeville to Miss Ann Martha, daughter of C. Gaillard, Esq., of Anderson District.

Issue of April 16, 1834
Married on the 20th February last, by the Rev. B. R. Bray, Mr. Alexander W. Mitchell of Henry Co., Ga., to Miss Martha, eldest daughter of Mr. Philip M'Daniel of DeKalb Co., Geo., formerly of Anderson District, S. C.
Married on the 1st inst., by William Oliver, Esq., Mr. John Neale to Miss Malinda Weems, all of Pickens District.

Issue of April 30, 1834
    Married on the 22d inst., by Rev. Richard B. Cater, Mr. F. F. Beattie
to Miss Emily E. Hamlin, all of Greenville.
    Died at Clarksville, Geo., on the 22d inst., Mr. John S. Monroe, for-
merly of this District.

Issue of May 7, 1834
    Married on Thursday evening, the 1st of May, by the Rev. D. Hutchins,
Mr. Ezekiel Stanley, to Miss Margaret, daughter of Robert Holland, Esq.,
of Anderson District.

Issue of May 14, 1834
    Married yesterday evening, by the Rev. Richard B. Cater, Mr. Edwin
Reese to Miss Sarah Ann, daughter of Col. Richard Lewis, decd.

Issue of May 28, 1834
    Married yesterday evening by Rev. A. W. Ross, Dr. A. H. Reese to Miss
Jane A., eldest daughter of Mr. Samuel Cherry.
    Married on Thursday evening last, by Rev. W. Anthony, Mr. William
M'Crary to Miss Nancy, daughter of Mr. Jeremiah Wilson, all of Anderson
District.
    Died on the 20th inst., at the residence of Mr. Samuel Maverick, near
this place, Mr. Joseph T. Weyman, formerly of Charleston.

Issue of June 11, 1834
    Married on Wednesday evening last, in this village, by Rev. Richard B.
Cater, Mr. William M. Ferrell to Miss Nancy T., daughter of Mr. Thomas
Lorton, decd.
    Married on Thursday evening at Silver Glade, the residence of Gen. J.
B. Earle, by the same, Mr. Archibald C. Campbell to Miss Emily Hannon.
    Married on Thursday last, by James C. Griffin, Esq., Mr. James Tuffnel,
aged 85, to Miss Elizabeth Earle, aged about 50.

Issue of July 2, 1834
    Married on Thursday, the 19th inst., by the Rev. Sandford Vandiver,
Mr. Thomas E. Ware, of Abbeville District, to Miss Mary, only daughter of
Capt. Adam Jones, of Greenville District.

Issue of July 23, 1834
    Died at Ft. Gaines, on the 7th inst., Mr. Elias Earle, son of Samuel
Earle, late of this District (eulogy).

Issue of August 6, 1834
    Died on the 2nd inst., Sydney Brownlow, aged 21 years.

Issue of August 20, 1834
    Married on the 15th inst., by Rev. Wm. Carlile, Mr. Bartholomew J.
Cannon, to Miss Arminda C. Tucker, both of Anderson.

Issue of September 24, 1834
    Married on Thursday evening last, by Rev. Drury Hutchins, Mr. Simon C.
Doyle, to Miss Mahala, daughter of Thomas Townsend, Esq., all of Anderson
District.
    Judge Wm. H. Crawford died in the vicinity of Elberton on his way to
preside at the September term of Court of Elbert Co. Aug. Chron.
    Elias Horry, Esq., died yesterday afternoon in this city. Char Courier.

Issue of October 1, 1834
    Married on the 28th inst., by Andrew J. Liddell, Esq., Mr. John C.
Miller of Pickens to Mrs. Sarah Ledbetter of Anderson.

Issue of October 15, 1834
    Died at Taladega, Ala, on the 20th ult., Thomas Hallum, eldest son of
the widow Jane Hallum of Pickens District, S. C. (eulogy).

Issue of October 29, 1834
    Married on the 14th October, by William Oliver, Esq., Mr. Andrew Wimes
of Ga., to Miss Martha Neale of Pickens District.
    Married on the 23d October, by Wm Oliver, Esq., Mr. William Crenshaw,
to Miss Elizabeth Grant, all of Pickens District.

Married on Thursday the 16th inst., by Rev. William Magee, Mr. George S. Smith, to Miss Elizabeth, daughter of Mr. William Hunt, both of Anderson District.

Issue of November 5, 1834
Married last evening by the Rev. Mr. Cater, Mr. George T. Anderson to Miss Susan M. Jenkins, all of this District.

Died Wednesday evening, the 29th ult., in Pickens District, Capt. Davis Sloan, in the 48th year of his age...a native of our district... member of the Baptist Church...left a widow and family of children.

Issue of November 26, 1834
Died in Pickens District, on the 20th inst., Mr. William Willson, in the 84th year of his age, having survived his second partner in life by 17 days.

Issue of December 3, 1834
Married on Thursday evening, Nov. 27, by the Rev. William Magee, Mr. Wiley Lattimer of Abbeville to Miss Irena S., youngest daughter of Hezekiah Rice, Esq., of Anderson District.

Departed this life on Tuesday, the 25th inst., James Stuart, second and only son of W. J. and Serena Knauff, aged 11 months and 27 days.

Issue of December 17, 1834
Married on Tuesday evening, the 2nd inst., Mr. Thomas Cucksworth, to Miss Sarah Guiton, both of Anderson District.

Married on Tuesday evening, the 9th inst., by Wm Hunter, Esq., Mr. Elisha Dean to Miss Caroline, daughter of Mr. James Parson, all of Pickens District.

Issue of December 24, 1834
Married on Tuesday last, by Rev. James Stacey, Mr. Jesse Ingram to Miss Francis Newton, both of Anderson District.

Issue of January 7, 1835
Married on Tuesday evening last, by the Rev. Mr. Carlile, Mr. George Graham of Newberry district, to Mrs. Martha Skelton, of Anderson District.

Died on the 28th inst., at his residence in Anderson, Mr. Daniel R. Towers, in the 36th year of his age...leaving a wife a 6 children...member of the Presbyterian Church.

Issue of January 21, 1835
Married on the 17th ult., by Rev. D. Humphreys, Mr. Francis Young to Miss Elvira Caldwell.

Married on the 23d ult., by the same, Mr. Joseph Hutchison, to Miss Flora McDonald, both of Elbert Co., Ga.

Married on the 1st inst., by the same, Mr. John Rice of Anderson, to Miss Nancy Allen of Abbeville District.

Issue of January 28, 1835
Married on Thursday, the 15th inst., by the Rev. William Carlile, Mr. Samuel B. Alexander to Miss Dianna W. Hopkins.

Married on Tuesday evening, the 20th inst., by the same, Mr. John L. Low to Miss Rebecca Anderson.

Died on the morning of the 22d inst., Mr. Charles Story in the 69th year of his age...a native of Sumter District, and for the last 20 years, a citizen of this District, and elder in the Presbyterian Church.

Issue of February 13, 1835
Died on the 2nd inst., James Richard, infant son and only child of Richard T. Wilson, aged 1 month and 28 days.

Married on the evening of the 3d inst., by the Rev. Mr. Carlile, Mr. Elisha B. Lewis to Miss Martha M. Pool.

Married on Sunday the 18th inst., by A. O. Norris, Esq., Mr. James W. Davis to Miss Mary Wood, all of Anderson District.

Issue of February 20, 1835
Married in Pickens District, on the 1 January last, by Wm Barton, Esq., Mr. O. W. Trimmier to Miss Catherine, daughter of Mr. Robert Ballew-

Married in Habersham Co., Ga., on the 12th inst., by _____ Taylor, Esq., Mr. M. T. Trimmier to Miss Rachel C., daughter of Mr. John Pulliam.

Issue of March 6, 1835

Married at Varrennes, on the 10th ult., by the Rev. Mr. Carlile, Mr. Samuel Bell to Miss Anna Stevenson.

Married on the evening of the 1st inst., by the same, Mr. Amos Acker, to Miss Lucy C. Davis.

Death of Mr. William Turpin, formerly of S. C., but for some years past a resident of New York, completed more than four score years, died on the 21st ult.

Issue of March 20, 1835

Married on the 10th March, by Wm. Oliver, Esq., Mr. John Cobb to Miss Isabella Copeland, at Blakely.

Issue of March 27, 1835

Married on Thursday, the 12th inst., by the Rev. William Magee, Mr. Mason Kay, to Miss Mary Cox, both of Anderson.

Issue of April 3, 1835

Married on the 17th ult., near Hamburg, by the Rev. Henry Reid, Mr. John C. Kilpatrick Jun., of this District ot Miss Eliza Amanda, daughter of Col. Benjamin F. Whitner, of the former place.

Issue of April 10, 1835

Married on March 17, Mr. David M'Carly to Miss Nancy M'Kay.

Married on March 26, Mr. James M'Daniel to Miss Elvira Pickens.

Married on April 2, Mr. J. J. M'Lees to Miss Mary Skelton by the Rev. D. Humphreys.

Issue of May 1, 1835

Mrs. Nancy T. Ferrell, consort of Wm. M. Ferrell, departed this life, Wednesday last in the 24th year of her age...member of the Presbyterian Church.

Issue of May 8, 1835

Died at his residence near this place on 5 May, Thomas L. Dart... member of the Episcopal Church.

Issue of May 22, 1835

Married on Thursday evening, the 14th May, by Rev. Samuel Gibson, Mr. Lewis Dupre of Anderson, to Miss Amanda Malvina Rhodes, of Greenville.

Married on Sunday evening the 10th inst., by Rev. Mr. Anthony, Mr. Danton Browne to Miss Louisa Posey.

Married on Tuesday evening, the 12th inst., by the same, Mr. John Duncan to Miss Hester Mary, daughter of Elijah Browne, Esq.

Married on Thursday evening, the 14th inst., by F. S. Norris, Esq., Mr. William Gregg to Miss Caroline Wiatt, both of Anderson District.

Issue of June 5, 1835

Married on Tuesday, the 26th ult., by Rev. Sanford Vandiver, Mr. Stephen S. Lattimer of Abbeville to Miss Amelia C., youngest daughter of Mr. Josiah Thompson, decd., of Greenville District.

Issue of August 7, 1835

Married on the 4th inst., by Wm. M'Murry, Esq., Mr. Russel Crawford of Georgia, to Miss Nancy, daughter of John Williams of Anderson District.

Died on the 8th ult., Mrs. Jane Hubbard, in the 77th year of her age.

Issue of September 4, 1835

Died on Wednesday, the 29th July, Mrs. Nancy Ann Archer, consort of Mr. John Archer, in the 50th year of her age...left a husband and 7 children...buried at Mount Tabor Church, discourse & prayer by Rev. James Burroughs.

Died on Saturday, the 29th ult., aged about 69 years, Samuel H. Dickson, Esq., some years since, a member of the Senatorial & Representative branches of the Legislature of this State.

Died in this place, on the 31st ult., Thos. Larton, infant son of W. M. Ferrell, aged 4 months and 17 days.

Issue of September 11, 1835
Married on the 20th August, in the town of Monroe, Ga., by the Rev. William Choice, Mr. Ira O. M'Daniel of Greene Co., Ga., to Miss Pebecca Jane, eldest daughter of Maj. Daniel Walker, of Monroe.
Married on Tuesday the 1st inst., by Rev. Wm. M'Gee, Mr. John Conn, of Anderson, to Miss Martha Allen, of Abbeville District.
Died on the 25th August last, near Athens, Tenn., in the 62d year of her age, Mrs. Frances Owen, formerly of this District. (eulogy).

Issue of September 18, 1835
Married on Tuesday evening last, by Rev. R. B. Cater, Dr. James W. Earle, of Greenville, to Miss Amanda M., daughter of Mr. E. B. Renson, of this village.

Issue of October 2, 1835
Married in this place on Wednesday, the 16th September by Rev. Robert Nall, Mr. L. Y. Tarrant of Marion, to Miss Elizabeth Griffin, daughter of James C. Griffin, of Pendleton, S. C. Marion (Ala) Mercury.

Issue of October 16, 1835
Died at his residence near Anderson C. H., on the 1st inst., Peter Keys, Esq., in the 70th year of his age. The deceased was a native of Ireland, and long a respectable inhabitant of this state...left a widow and large family.

Issue of October 23, 1835
Departed this life October 3, Mrs. Martha Clark, consort of Matthew Clark, of Anderson District, aged 66 years...member of the Methodist Episcopal Church...(eulogy).
Married on Tuesday evening, the 13th inst., by Rev. Wm. Carlile, Mr. Thomas George to Miss Nancy Matilda Wilson, daughter of Mr. Charles Wilson.

Issue of November 6, 1835
Died on Monday the 2d inst., William, infant son of Dr. Wm. and Mary P. Anderson, aged 4 months.

Issue of November 20, 1835
Married by Joseph Cox, Esq., on the 8th inst., Mr. Alexander Simpson to Miss Cassey Davis.

Issue of November 27, 1835
Married on the 19th inst., by Rev. Thomas Dawson, Mr. Tho. K. Hamilton to Miss Teresa O'Barr, daughter of Polly O'Barr, both of this district.

Issue of December 18, 1835
Married by Wm. M'Murry, Esq., on Sunday evening last, Mr. Aaron Sherriff to Miss Sarah Whitten, daughter of John Whitten, decd., all of Anderson District.
Married in this village, on Sunday evening last, by the Rev. Jesse Mercer, Mr. James W. Price, Printer, to Miss S. H. Johnson, all of this place. Washington News, Dec.3.
Married in Lincoln County [Georgia] on Monday evening last, by the Rev. Jesse Mercer, Mr. William A. Mercer, editor of the News, to Miss Mary Ann Walker, daughter of Rev. John H. Walker.

Issue of December 25, 1835
Married on Tuesday evening last, by Wm Hunter, Esq., Mr. Berry Davis to Miss Pamela, daughter of John O. Smith, all of Pickens District.

Issue of January 1, 1836
Married on the 17th ult., by Rev. Wm. G. Mullinix, Mr. Isaac M. Newton to Miss Anna Ingram, all of Anderson District.

Issue of January 22, 1836
Married on Thursday the 14th inst., by Rev. Mr. Kennedy, Mr. William Poe of Augusta, Ga., to Miss Ellen, daughter of Col. Jos. Taylor, of this district.
Married on Tuesday evening, the 5th inst., by the Rev. William Magee, Mr. Joshua S. Acker of Anderson District, to Miss Matilda S., daughter of Mr. John Williams of Greenville District.

Also by the same, on Thursday evening, the 7th, William Davis to Miss Jane, daughter of Mr. Wm Kay sen., both of this district.

Married on Sunday evening, the 10th inst., by the same, Capt. William P. Hunnicutt, to Miss Elizabeth Clinkscales, all of this district.

Also, by the same, on Thursday, the 14th, Mr. William S. Hunt, to Miss Elizabeth Braswell, all of this District.

Also on the same evening, by the same, Mr. Michael Magee of Abbeville District, to Miss Sophronia Shumate, of Greenville District.

Issue of January 29, 1836

Married by Wm. M'Murry on the 7th inst., Mr. William M. Willson of Anderson District, to Miss Martha, daughter of Bagle(?) Nalley, of Pickens District.

Married by the same, on the 14th, Capt. Benjamin Dilworth to Miss Adaline, daughter of John Norris, decd., all of Anderson District.

Issue of February 5, 1836

Gen. John B. Earle, Adj. Gen. of S. C., died at his residence in this district on Wednesday last, at 3 P. M. Gen. Earle was born, we believe, in N. C., and at his death was in the 70th year of his age.

Issue of February 26, 1836

Married on the 26th ult., by Rev. P. Humphreys, Mr. Obadiah Dean to Miss Elizabeth M'Pherson.

Married on the 28th ult., by Wm. M'Murry, Esq., Mr. James Oliver to Miss Clarissa, daughter of Mr. John Willson, decd, all of Anderson Dist.

Married on Thursday evening, the 4th inst., by Rev. Wm. Magee, Mr. Wiley Davis to Miss Levina K., daughter of Mr. Isaac Cox, decd., all of this District.

Issue of April 1, 1836

Died at her residence in Anderson District, on the 25th March, Mrs. Ann Hamilton, wife of Thomas Hamilton in her 75th year. They have lived together as partners upwards of 50 years. They raised a large family, with several orphans...(eulogy).

Issue of April 8, 1836

Died on the 10th March, at her residence in Alabama, Mrs. Rebecca Dickson, widow of Samuel H. Dickson, Esq., late of this district, aged about 60 years.

Issue of April 15, 1836

Died at his residence in Pickens District, on Friday last, Robert M. Briggs, Esq. Mr. B. was an officer in the U. S. Army in the War of 1812.

Issue of April 29, 1836

Married on April 7, by Rev. D. Humphreys, Mr. James C. Keys to Miss Louisa D. Lewis, youngest daughter of Major Lewis.

Married by the same, Mr. Samuel Caldwell, to Miss Mary Cox, all of Anderson District.

Married on the 22nd March by Rev. B. D. DuPre, Maj. Thos J. Humphreys to Miss Towers, all of Pickens District.

Died on the 21st inst., at her residence near this place, Mrs. Floride Colhoun, relict of the late Hon. John Ewing Colhoun, aged 71 years.

Issue of May 6, 1836

Died on 2 March in Pickens District, Mrs. Susan M'Guffin, in the 82d year of her age.

Issue of May 13, 1836

Married in Edgefield District, on the 3d of May by Rev. _____, Robert Creswell, Esq., of Laurens (formerly of this district), to Miss Rebecca, daughter of Elihu Bullock, decd.

Died in Anderson District, April 14, at her residence, Mrs. Barbara M'Allister, wife of Nathan M'Alister, aged 65.

Issue of May 27, 1836

Married in Washington City, on the 5th inst., by Rev. Mr. Hawley, Andrew P. Calhoun, Esq., of South Carolina, to Miss Margaret M., daughter of Gen. Duff Green.

50

Died at New York, on the 4th inst., Bentley Hasell, Esq., of Montgomery, Ala., formerly of this District.

Issue of June 17, 1836
Married on Tuesday the 7th inst., by Rev. A. W. Ross, Mr. James D.
Wright of Pickens District, to Miss Elizabeth Clanahan, of Anderson Dist.
Departed this life on 8 May, Gen. Ira Griffin, of Mobile, in the 37th
year of his age. He was a native of this district, and son of James C.
Griffin, Esq. He emigrated to Alabama and settled in Tuscaloosa about
18 years ago. A few years back, married a daughter of Thomas Tarrant,
formerly of Greenville District, and removed to Mobile, where he died.
Mary Harris, wife of John Harris, and eldest daughter of Gen. Andrew
Pickens, departed this life on 27 May 1836...member of the Presbyterian
Church.
Died on Saturday, the 4th inst., at the residence of his father in
this district, Rev. J. F. C. Harris, in the 21st year of his age. He was
admitted to membership of the Methodist Episcopal Church at age 15, and
licenced at age 19.

Issue July 8, 1836
Married on Thursday, the 30th ult., by the Rev. David Humphreys, Mr.
James Taylor of Oglethorpe Co., Ga., to Miss Caroline, daughter of Mr.
James Connel of Anderson District, S. C.
Died in Montgomery Co., N. C., on the 26th ult., Col. James R. Ervin,
a member of the Senate of this State from Chesterfield district.
Died on the 24th February last, at his residence in Cornersville,
Giles Co., Tenn., in the 47th year of his age, Ephraim M. Massey, Esq.,
a native of Pendleton District, S. C.
Isaac Motte Dart, only son of the late Dr. Thomas L. Dart, died in the
15th year of his age. He leaves a widowed mother and five orphan sisters.

Issue of July 15, 1836
Married on Tuesday evening, the 5th inst., by James Gilmer, Esq., Mr.
Thomas Shelton to Miss Tamer Minton, all of Anderson District.

Issue of August 5, 1836
Married on Tuesday evening, the 12th July, by Jas Gilmer, Esq., Mr.
James Gaines to Miss Jane, daughter of Mr. Andrew Seawright, all of Ander-
son District.

Issue of August 12, 1836
Married on last evening, by the Rev. D. Humphreys, Dr. Andrew P.
Cater of Anderson to Miss Martha C., daughter of Mr. E. P. Benson, of
this place.
Married on Thursday evening, the 4th inst., by the Rev. Wm. Carlisle,
Mr. Taply Anderson to Miss Louisa, daughter of George Manning, Esq.

Issue of September 2, 1836
Married on Thursday evening, the 18 of August, by Rev. S. Vandiver,
Mr. Milton Hicks, to Miss Francis, daughter of Mr. Larkin Wright, both
of Anderson District.
Also on Tuesday evening, the 23d of August, by the same, Mr. Jesse
C. Magee, to Miss Sarah M. H., daughter of Mr. W. P. Nelson, both of And-
erson District.
Married on the 19th July, by Rev. David Humphreys, Capt. Pickens Mc-
Lin, to Miss Ann Simpson.
Married on the 18th July by the same, Mr. Laban Car to Miss Louisa
Brooks.

Issue of September 16, 1836
Married in Tuscaloosa, Ala., on the 4th ult., Samuel H. Maverick,
Esq., formerly of this place, to Miss Mary A. Adams.

Issue of September 30, 1836
Married on the evening of the 1st of September by John Myers, Esq.,
Mr. Allen Lanear, to Miss Mary Ann, daughter of Mr. Allen Guest, both of
Pickens District.
Married on the evening of the 8th September by the Rev. David Hum-
phreys, Mr. Jno. W. B. Skelton to Miss Eliza, daughter of Mr. Aaron
Vandiver, all of Anderson District.

Married on the same evening by _____ Barton, Esq., Mr. Jackson Lowry,
to Miss Catherine Harrison, both of Anderson District.

Issue of October 21, 1836
      Died on the 15th September in Mississippi, in the 26th year of his
age, Mr. George W. Verner, formerly of Pickens District.

Issue of November 11, 1836
      Died on Wednesday morning last at about 3 o'clock, Mrs. Maria Ander-
son, relict of the late Col. Robert Anderson, of this District.

Issue of November 18, 1836
      Died at the residence of the widow Acker near Pierce's ford on Saluda
in Anderson District, on the 5th inst., Mrs. Elizabeth Halbert, within
a few weeks of 90 years of age...member of the Baptist Church. She raised
13 children who are scattered in the several states of Indiana, Missouri,
Mississippi, Alabama, Tennessee, and this state.

Issue of December 9, 1836
      Married on Sunday evening, the 30th October in Pickens District, by
the Rev. Hiram Lecroy, Mr. Jobhery Merritt to Miss Lucinda, daughter of
Pendleton Isabel.
      Married on Tuesday the 7th of November, in Pickens District by Rev.
Drury Hutchins, Mr. G. W. Treadaway, to Miss Harriet, daughter of Frederick Moss.
      Married on Thursday evening, the 24th of November, in Anderson Dist-
rict., by the Rev. Dr. Lewis, Mr. William H. Barry to Miss Harriet,
daughter of Mr. David Cambrell.
      Also on Tuesday evening, the 29th November, at Fair Play, by the Rev.
D. Hutchins, Mr. M. S. M'Cay, to Miss Martha P. Collins.

Issue of December 30, 1836
      Married on Tuesday evening last by Rev. Mr. Dannelly, Maj. Richard
T. Simpson of Laurens, to Miss Margaret M. Taliaferro, of this district.
      Married on the same evening, by the Rev. Mr. Moss, Mr. Warren Knight,
to Miss Amanda Robinson, of this district.

Issue of January 6, 1837
      Married on the 21st December by Wm. M'Murry, Esq., Mr. John Owen, to
Miss Catharine, daughter of Mr. Frederick Owen, of Anderson District.

Issue of January 13, 1837
      Departed this life, Dec. 27, 1836, George Ann, daughter of Mrs. Mary
Dart, aged 7 years and 2 months.

Issue of January 20, 1837
      Married on Wednesday evening, the 18th inst., by Rev. William Magee,
Mr. Beaufort W. Burns, to Miss Nancy, daughter of the late Robert Isbell,
both of Anderson District.
      Married on Tuesday evening by Rev. Mr. Kennedy, Mr. Alexander Waddell
to Miss Sarah Ann, daughter of Mr. James Henderson of Pickens District.

Issue of February 3, 1837
      Married on the 22nd of December, by the Rev. D. Humphreys, Mr. Laurens
F. Baker to Miss Rebecca Martin, both of Greenville District.
      Married by the same, Mr. John M. Simpson, to Miss Mary Harris, both of
Anderson District.
      Married by the same, on the 10th of January, Dr. S. Williams to Miss
Fair, both of Abbeville District.
      Married by the same, Mr. Andrew Joice to Miss Louisa Gunnels, both of
Greenville District.
      Married on the 17th of January, by the Rev. James Hembree, Mr. James
O'Kelly of Elbert County, Ga., to Miss Sarah Master, of Anderson District.
      Married on the 26th of January by Rev. Wm. Magee, Dr. Abner E. Fant
of Fairfield District, to Miss Elizabeth O., daughter of Ch's Stark, Esq.,
of Abbeville District.

Issue of February 10, 1837
      Married on the 29th January by Rev. W. G. Mullinix, Mr. John R. Web-
ster of Georgia to Miss Mary S. Casey of Pickens District.

Issue of February 17, 1837
    Married on Thursday the 9th inst., by Rev. Wm. Magee, Mr. Jacob R.
Cox, of Pickens District, to Miss Jane Emaline, daughter of Rev. Sanford
Vandiver of Anderson District.
    Married, also on Tuesday evening, the 7th inst., by Rev. David Simmons,
Capt. A. B. Harris, to Miss Winney, daughter of John Gordon, both of
Anderson District.

Issue of February 24, 1837
    Married on the 9th inst., by Rev. Wm Mullinix, Mr. John W. Harbin to
Miss Jane C. M'Clure of Anderson District.

Issue of March 10, 1837
    Married on Thursday evening, the 16th February by Rev. D. Hutchins,
Mr. Samuel Isbell of Pickens to Miss Ellen, daughter of Mr. William King
of Anderson District.
    Married on Sunday evening, the 26th February, by Rev. Levi Garrison,
Mr. Cannady White of Franklin Co., Ga., to Miss Maria Harris, of Anderson
District, S. C.

Issue of March 17, 1837
    Married on Thursday evening, the 9th inst., by Rev. D. Humphreys, Mr.
William D. Steele to Miss Margaret, daughter of Mr. Archibald M'Elroy,
both of Anderson District.

Issue of March 24, 1837
    Married on March the 16th by Rev. Wm. G. Mullinix, Mr. Aaron Boggs
to Miss Matilda Gaines, all of Pickens District.

Issue of March 31, 1837
    Married on the 21st inst., by William Oliver, Esq., Mr. Greenbury
Heaton to Miss Rilla Crow, all of Pickens.

Issue of April 7, 1837
    Married on Thursday evening, the 5th ult., by J. S. Magee, Esq., Mr.
Daniel Birket, to Miss Catherine Woolbright, all of Pickens District.

Issue of April 14, 1837
    Married on Thursday evening, the 6th inst., by Rev. WM. Magee, Mr.
William J. Taylor to Miss Frances Keaton.

Issue of April 21, 1837
    Married on the 16th March by Rev. D. Humphreys, Mr. Robert M. Morton
to Miss Rebecca Pedan, all of Greenville District.
    Departed this life on Tuesday morning, the 11th inst., between 5 and
6 o'clock, Capt. James Mattison, in the 35th year of his age...left a
consort and three children.
    Departed this life on Saturday the 1st of April after a protracted
illness, in the 44th year of her age, Mrs. Elizabeth Fant, consort of
Valentine D. Fant, Esq., of this district....daughter of William Nevitt
of Fairfield District, where she was raised, married and lived until the
removal a few years ago, of her now bereft husband to this district. She
was the mother of four little sons...member of the Baptist Church.

Issue of April 28, 1837
    Married on Thursday evening, the 20th inst., by the Rev. Wm. Magee,
Mr. John K. Harkness to Miss T. Amanda Magee, daughter of Mr. John Magee.

Issue of May 12, 1837
    Married on Tuesday evening, the 25th of April last, by Joel E. Welborn,
Esq., Mr. Charles L. Humphreys, formerly of Pickens District, to Miss
Clarinda, daughter of Thos. Crear, of Anderson District.
    Died on the 5th inst., at the residence of her son (Mr. Rob't Maxwell)
Mrs. Mary Carruth, in the 71st year of her age.

Issue of May 19, 1837
    Married on Saturday morning, the 13th inst., by Geo. Swilling, Esq.,
Mr. Alexander Geddis to Miss Cynthia Davis, all of Anderson District.

Issue of May 26, 1837
    Died at his residence in this district, on Friday morning, the 19th inst., Col. Lewelling Goode, recently a member of the Legislature of this State...left a widow with large family.
    Died on Wednesday the 3d inst., Mrs. Scott, consort of Mr. John Scott. And on Tuesday the 12th inst., Mr. Scott himself departed this life, in the 95th year of his age. He was one of those who fought for the liberties we are now enjoying...member of the Presbyterian Church.

Issue of June 2, 1837
    Married by Rev. D. Humphreys, May 16th, Mr. Charles M'Gregor to Miss Amanda M'Pherson, of Anderson District.

Issue of June 9, 1837
    Departed this life on the evening of the 3rd inst., Miss Lydia C. Stark, daughter of Charles Stark, Esq., of Abbeville District, in the 25th year of her age...leaves father, mother, 3 sisters, and one brother.

Issue of June 16, 1837
    Married on Sunday evening, the 11th inst., by the Rev. S. Vandiver, Valentine D. Fant, Esq., to Miss Esther Moore, both of Anderson District.
    Married on Tuesday the 11th inst., by Miles M. Norton, Esq., Mr. Elijah M'Gill of Anderson, to Miss Fanny Dodd of Pickens District.
    Departed this life on the 1st inst., Samuel McGill, of this District, in the 22nd year of his age....He had appeared before the So. Car. Presbytery at the last session, and after examination on experimental religion and his motives for entering the Gospel Ministry, he was unanimously received.

Issue of June 23, 1837
    Died on the 9th inst., near this place, Mr. Francis Burt sen., aged 78. Mr. B. was a native of Virginia, but came early in life to this state....member of the Baptist Church.
    Died in Pickens District, on Wednesday night, the 14th inst., Mrs. Susan Anderson, widow of Henry H. Anderson, decd, in the 23rd year of her age.

Issue of July 7, 1837
    Died in this village on Sunday morning, the 25th June last, Maj. Nathaniel Harris, in the 43rd year of his age...member of the Presbyterian Church.
    Departed this life on the morning of the 29th of June, Clarinda F. W., infant daughter of Capt. J. P. & Teresa C. Reed, aged 3 months and 20 days.

Issue of July 28, 1837
    Married on Thursday, the 13th inst., by Rev. S. Vandiver, Mr. Alfred M. Neal, of Elbert, Georgia, to Miss Cynthia M., daughter of Capt. David Watson, of Anderson, S. C.
    Departed this life on 19 July 1837, at Rockfield, the seat of Judge Prioleau near Pendleton, S. C., Miss Harriott Cleland Hamilton, in her 39th year, the youngest daughter of the late Major James Hamilton.
    Died at the residence of Maj. Seaborn, in Greenville District, on Friday, the 21st inst., Thomas Harrison, Esq., in the 47th year of his age. He was Treasurer and Comptroller General. He had served occasionally in the Legislature.
    From the Danville (Va.) Reporter, May 26.
Died in this place, on Wednesday morning, the 24th inst., Rev. William C. M'Elroy, Pastor of the Presbyterian Church in this place.

Issue of August 4, 1837
    Died on Sunday evening, the 30th ult., Mrs. Avis Symms, in the 71st year of her age. She was a native of Rhode Island, but for near half a century had resided at the place where she died in this district.
    Another Revolutionary Patriot Gone!
    Departed this life on Thursday morning, the 20th July, Mr. Edward Vandiver sen., aged 88 years. The deceased was a native of Virginia, and emigrated to Fairfield District, in 1768, where he lived until 1795, at which time he removed to Pendleton District. He fought under Gen. Greene at Eutaw Springs. He was the father of 21 children by two wives

(ten by the first wife whom he lost by death in Fairfield, and eleven by the second wife, whom he married after his removal to Pendleton.) He has 12 sons now living, six of whom are Baptist Preachers.

Issue of August 11, 1837
Married on Thursday the 1st August, by Wm. McMurry, Esq., Mr. Mason Leboon of Georgia, to Miss Emily, daughter of Mr. Benjamin Mullikin of Anderson.

Died on the 3d inst., John Ewing, second son of Col. J. E. Colhoun, aged 5 years and nearly two months.

Died at Columbus, Miss., on the 17th ult., Mr. Edmund M. Covington, late of Abbeville, aged 26.

Issue of August 18, 1837
Married on Thursday morning, the 20th ult., by Ja's. Gilmer, Esq., Mr. John Robinson to Miss Rhoda Holley, all of Anderson District.

Departed this life at Pendleton Village, on the 15th inst., William Choice Goodlett, youngest son of the late John H. Goodlett, Esq., decd., aged 6 years and 10 months.

Issue of August 25, 1837
Married on the 3rd August by Rev. D. Humphreys, Capt. Wilson Peadon to Miss Jane Thompson, both of Greenville District.

Married on the 16th of August, by the same, Mr. Matthew Snipes, to Miss Elizabeth McCoun, both of this District.

Died on the 14th of August, at his residence, Rock Mills, Anderson District, in the 66th year of his age, Major Lewis sen. The deceased was born in the State of Virginia, Loudon, Co., but early emigrated to this District....At his death, he held the office of Commissioner of Locations.

Issue of September 1, 1837
Married on the 28th of May, by Young Davis, Esq., Alexander Carver, to Miss Sarah, daughter of Richard Coggins, both of Pickens District.

Married on the 1st of June, by the same, Mr. Philip Weaks to Miss Sarah Wheeler, both of Habersham Co., Ga.

Issue of September 15, 1837
Married on the 3rd inst., by the Rev. W. G. Mullinix, Mr. James N. Arnold to Miss Mabry C., daughter of Mr. Hundley Evatt, all of Pickens.

Married on the 5th inst., by the same, Mr. Isaac M. Swords of Alabama, to Miss Catherine Newton of Anderson.

Died on Monday morning last, Mr. William P. M'Dow, leaving a wife with an infant family. (eulogy)

Died on Tuesday night, Mr. William Owen...left a widow and helpless family.

And on yesterday morning, _____, daughter of the above named Mr. Owen, aged about 4 or 5 years, departed this life.

Issue of September 22, 1837
Married at Friendville near Pendleton Village, by Rev. W. T. Potter, Paul Hamilton, Esq., to Miss Catharine A. Campbell, youngest daughter of the Rev. J. B. Campbell.

Issue of September 29, 1837
Married on the 12th inst., at La Fayette, Ala., Mr. Giles C. Pitts, to Miss Mary F. Adams, formerly of this place.

Issue of October 13, 1837
Married on Tuesday, the 3rd inst., by Wm. McMurry, Esq., Mr. Jackson Floyd to Miss Harriet, daughter of Stephen Ford, all of Anderson District.

Issue of October 20, 1837
Married on the 12th inst., by Rev. Sanford Vandiver, Mr. Joseph B. Jones, to Miss Harriet E., second daughter of William Berry, both of Anderson District.

Married on the 21st of September, by Rev. D. Humphreys, Mr. Solomon Seaborn Jones, to Miss Mary Moore Sadler, both of Elbert Co., Ga.

Issue of October 27, 1837
Married on the 12th inst., by Rev. W. G. Mullinix, Mr. Robert McCane

of Georgia, to Miss Mary Hallum of Pickens District.
Married on the 22d inst., by the same, Mr. Andrew Elrod, to Miss
Lucinda Morris, both of Anderson.

Issue of November 3, 1837
Married on the 26th October by the Rev. W. G. Mullinix, Mr. James J.
McClure to Miss Marilda C. Crist, both of Anderson.
Married on Tuesday the 24th ult., by Jesse S. McGee, Esq., Mr. Philip
Smith, to Miss Minerva, daughter of Abner Honea, all of Pickens District.
Died in this village, on the 24th ult., Mrs. Elizabeth Whitner, in the
69th year of her age...member of the Presbyterian Church.
Deceased, the 17th of October, after a short illness, Mary Elizabeth,
daughter of Wm. J. and Serena Knauff, aged 2 years, 6 months, and 10 days.

Issue of November 10, 1837
Married on Thursday evening, the 2nd inst., by Rev. W. Magee, Mr.
Josiah J. Ballentine, to Miss Amanda, eldest daughter of Mr. James Telford,
all of Anderson District.
Died on the 24th ult., after a short illness, Mrs. Hannah Baldwin,
wife of Stephen Baldwin, of Pickens District...member of the Baptist
Church...left a husband and large family of children.
And on the 31st her infant child, aged 11 months also departed this
life.

Issue of November 17, 1837
Married on the 7th inst., by the Rev. Mr. Ross, Mr. Thomas R. Cherry
to Miss Mary S. Harris, both of this village.

Issue of November 24, 1837
Married in Lafayette, Ala., on the 9th inst., by the Rev. Mr. Shelman,
Mr. Priestley Lawhon, formerly of this place, to Miss Mary Bostick.
Married on Tuesday evening, the 14th inst., by the Rev. M. M. Wallace,
Mr. John O. Grisham, to Miss Harriet T. Briggs, both of Pickens District.
Married on Tuesday last, the 21st inst., by W. L. Keith, Esq., Mr.
Tho's R. Price to Miss Ariel, eldest daughter of Abraham Stuart, all of
Pickens District.
Married on the 22nd inst., by Jesse S. M'Gee, Esq., Mr. Samuel Harris
to Miss Martha, daughter of James Young, all of Anderson District.
Died at his residence near Pendleton village, on the night of the 11th
inst., George Reed, in the 85th year of his age. The deceased served in
many expeditions and was engaged in many skirmished during the Revolutionary War...ruling Elder in the Presbyterian Church. An aged widow and
nine children survive.
Died on the 4th ult., Mr. David Hamilton, aged about 85.
Died on the 8th inst., Mr. Job Smith, aged 89. Both were soldiers of
the Revolution, and respectable citizens.
Died on the 9th inst., Dr. James Oliver, for many years a respectable
physician of this district.

Issue of December 1, 1837
Married on Tuesday evening, the 21st ult., by Rev. W. Magee, Mr. James
M. Vandiver of Anderson, to Miss Malinda S., daughter of Col. William
Ward of Abbeville District.
Died at his residence near Rock Mills, Anderson District, S. C., on
the 15th November, John Williford, in the 53d year of his age. Mr.
Williford had been travelling but a short time previous to his death
through the State of Georgia, and died from exposure. The deceased was
born in the State of North Carolina, Hartford (sic) County, and early
emigrated to the State of Georgia. After remaining there about 10 years,
he removed to this state.

Issue of December 15, 1837
Married on the 4th inst., by Rev. David Simmons, Mr. Zachariah Masters
to Miss Nancy Franks, daughter of Mrs. Edna Franks, both of Anderson Dist.
Married on the 21st November, by the Rev. D. Humprhies, Mr. Tho's
Stephenson to Miss Eliza Avery.
Married on the 7th December, by the same, Mr. Mark Prince, to Miss
Jane M'Cay.

Issue of December 22, 1837
Married on the 5th inst., by Rev. William Magee, Mr. Abner S. C.
Siddle to Miss Marilza A. Magee, all of this District.
Married on Thursday evening, the 14th inst., by the same, Mr. Levi
Burriss to Miss Teresa Caroline, daughter of Mr. John Stephenson, all of
Anderson District.

Issue of December 29, 1837
Married on the 21st inst., by Rev. Joseph Grisham, Mr. John B. Sitton
of Pendleton, to Miss Celenda, daughter of Col. J. Norton of Pickens Dist.
Married on the same evening, by the Rev. Drury Hutchins, Capt. George
W. Abbott to Miss Sarah, eldest daughter of Mrs. Margaret Cleveland, all
of Pickens District.
Married on the same evening, by the Rev. J. W. Lewis, Mr. _____ Coffee
to Miss Permelia, youngest daughter of Mrs. Sarah Isbell, all of Pickens
District.
Died at Fort Hill, on the 21st inst., John C. Calhoun, the infant son
of Mr. and Mrs. Andrew P. Calhoun, aged 7 months.

Issue of January 5, 1838
Married on Thursday evening, the 14th inst., by the Rev. S. Vandiver,
Mr. Thomas M. Vandiver to Miss SArah, daughter of Mr. Stephen Liverett,
both of Anderson District.
Married on the 26th December, by the Rev. W. G. Mullinax, Mr. Wm. C.
Elrod, to Miss Mary E. Rogers, both of Anderson District.

Issue of January 12, 1838
Married on Thursday evening, the 28th ult., by Rev. W. Magee, Mr. John
B. Smith, to Miss Mary Caroline, daughter of Mr. Aaron Dean, all of And-
erson District.
Married on Thursday the 4th inst., by the Rev. Sanford Vandiver, Mr.
Harrison Lattimer to Miss Mary Elvira, eldest daughter of Rev. Wm. Magee,
all of Anderson District.
Died suddenly on the 3d inst., Warren Davis, infant son of Col. J. E.
Colhoun, aged 16 months and 9 days.

Issue of January 19, 1838
Married on Tuesday evening, the 9th inst., by the Rev. Thos. Dawson,
Mr. John Crooks, to Miss Harriet Cleveland.
Married on the 14th inst., by the Rev. W. C. Mullinax, Rev. Tyre B.
Mauldin to Miss Elizabeth F. Gaines, all of Pickens.

Issue of February 2, 1838
Married on the 18th December by Rev. W. G. Mullinax, Mr. William Cox
of Georgia, to Miss Letty Garner, of Pickens District.
Married on Thursday evening, the 18th ult., by Jas. Gilmer, Esq., Mr.
Edmund Thacker to Miss Eleanor, daughter of Mr. James Driver, all of
Anderson District.
Died at home in this district, on the 9th ult., Mrs. Nancy M. Cunningham, wife of Mr. Thos. Cunningham, in her 26th year. In October, she
visited her father's (Mr. James Anderson) in Spartanburg. Spent some time
at Dr. Campbell's in Laurens. She left a husband and two little children
...(eulogy).

Issue of Feburary 16, 1838
Married on Thursday the 8th inst., by Wm. M'Murry, Esq., Mr. H. D.
M'Daniel, of Pickens District, to Miss Milley Kelly of Anderson District,
daughter of Mrs. Martha Kelly.

Issue of March 2, 1838
Married on Sunday evening, the 25th ult., by James Gilmer, Esq., Mr.
Dempsey Cox, to Miss Nancy, daughter of Mr. Daniel Thatcher, all of Ander-
son District.
Married on the 22d February by the Rev. W. C. Graves, Mr. Jacob B.
Perry to Miss Mary Ann, daughter of Rev. Philip Porter, all of Pickens
District.

Issue of March 23, 1838
Married on Sunday the 11th inst., by Wm. McMurry, Esq., Mr. Mathew
Dickson to Miss Martha Golding, daughter of W. Golding, all of Anderson
District.

Issue of March 30, 1838
    Married on Tuesday evening, the 8th ult., by the Rev. Wm. Magee, Mr.
Hugh S. Alexander, to Miss Malina Wyatt, both of this District.
    Married by the same, on Thursday evening, the 8th inst., Mr. Wm. F.
Clinkscales to Miss Rosy Ann Harkness, of this district.
    Married by the same, on Tuesday evening, the 13th inst., Mr. William
M. Paschal of Abbeville District, to Mrs. Eliza Burriss, of this District.

Issue of April 27, 1838
    Died on the 19th inst., Mr. Joseph Rhodes, a native of England, but
for a number of year, a resident of this country.

Issue of May 11, 1838
    Married in Clarksville, Ga., on Tuesday the 1st inst., by Rev. David
Ballew, Mr. Nicholas R. Bradshaw of Ashville, Alabama, to Miss Emily
Amanda Wallace of the former place.

Issue of May 18, 1838
    Married on the 19th April last, by the Rev. Mr. M'Cullough, Mr. Tho's
D. Bordeaux of Lauderdale, Miss., to Miss Laura, daughter of Richard Harris of Sumpter Co., Alabama, formerly of Pickens District, S. C.
    Death of Mr. William H. Craig, formerly of Pickens District, S. C. &
late of Pickens County, Alabama...shot (accidentally) on 17 April...in
the 54th year of his age.

Issue of May 25, 1838
    Married on the 20th inst., by W. L. Keith, Esq., Mr. Robert Stewart,
jun. to Miss Elizabeth, daughter of Daniel Durham, all of Pickens District.

Issue of June 1, 1838
    Married on May 10th, by Rev. Edwin Cater, Mr. W. Leveritt to Miss
Elizabeth A., only daughter of Mr. R. Prince, all of Anderson.

Issue of June 15, 1838
    Married on Thursday the 31st May, by Rev. Robert King, Mr. Ibzam Rice
to Miss Barbara, eldest daughter of Mr. Enoch Brazeal, all of Anderson.

Issue of June 22, 1838
    Married on Tuesday evening, the 12th inst., by Jas. Henderson, Esq.,
Mr. John H. King, to Miss Narcissa Day, of Pickens District.

Issue of June 29, 1838
    Departed this life on 21st inst., Mrs. Mary Dupre, aged 72 years and
9 months, wife of Benjamin Dupre (eulogy).

Issue of July 13, 1838
    Married on Tuesday evening, the 5th ult., by James Gilmer, Esq., Mr.
James Thacker to Miss Sarah, daughter of Mr. James Driver, all of
Anderson District.

Issue of July 20, 1838
    Married on Tuesday evening, the 10th inst., by the Rev. Thomas Dawson,
Mr. W. M. M. Gibson, recently of Northumberland County, England, to Miss
Rachel Margaret, daughter of Mr. Jesse Lewis of this district.

Issue of August 24, 1838
    Married on the 16th inst., by Rev. B. D. Dupre, Mr. Samuel Verner of
Pickens District, to Miss Melinda Crawford of Franklin Co., Ga.

Issue of August 31, 1838
    Married on the 21st inst., by Rev. D. Humphreys, Mr. M. Lewis to Miss
Sarah B., second daughter of Mr. G. Horton, all of Anderson District.

Issue of September 7, 1838
    Married on Thursday evening, the 30th ult., by Rev. W. G. Mullinix, Mr.
Richard I. Duncan, to Miss Matilda Ann Fowler, all of Anderson District.

Issue of September 14, 1838
    Died on the 12th June at Matagorda (Texas), Hugh D. Gaston, formerly
of Pendleton, S. C. leaving a youthful consort and two little children.

Departed this life on the 8th September 1838, at his residence in Pickens District, Mr. Tho. W. Carne, formerly of Charleston, S. C., aged 65 (eulogy).

Issue of September 28, 1838
Died at his residence in this district, on Sunday morning, the 23d inst., Mr. John Brewer, in the 53d year of his age...a member of the first Universalist Society in Anderson District from its organization to the time of his death...funeral address by Rev. Allen Fuller.

Issue of October 5, 1838
Married on Thursday the 27th ult., by Rev. W. Magee, Mr. Silas W. Kay to Miss Maranda B. Smith, all of Anderson District.
Married on the same evening, by the same, Mr. Nimrod Richey of Abbeville District, to Miss Ann Caroline, daughter of Mr. John Magee, of Anderson District.
Married on Sunday evening, the 30th ult., by Rev. David Simmons, Mr. Salathiel Bradberry, Jr. to Miss Margaret, daughter of Mr. James Fant, both of Anderson District.

Issue of October 19, 1838
Married on the 11th October by Rev. W, C. Mullinix, Mr. Leverit A. Osborn, to Miss Jane Hamilton, all of Pickens District.
Married on the 11th inst., by Rev. Drury Hutchins, Mr. Henry N. White of Anderson to Miss Nancy, daughter of Jesse Stribling, Esq., of Pickens District.
Married on the 4th October, by Rev. B. D. Dupre, Mr. Joab Wilson to Miss Martha E. M. Dupre, all of this District.

Issue of November 9, 1838
Married on the 18th October, by John Adair, Esq., Mr. Joab Gregg to Miss Mary Kelly.
Married on the 1st November, by the same, Henry Medford, to Miss Rachel Dorsey, all of Pickens District.

Issue of November 16, 1838
Married at Fort Hill near Pendleton, on the evening of the 13th inst., by Rev. Wm T. Potter, Thomas C. Clemson, Esq., to Miss Anne Maria, eldest daughter of the Hon. J. C. Calhoun.
Married on the 8th November, by the Rev. B. D. Dupre, Mr. Sydney Davis to Miss Mary Knox, all of Pickens District.

Issue of December 14, 1838
Married on the 12th inst., by the Rev. B. D. DuPre, Mr. Isaac Mc-Whorter to Miss Eliza Hill, all of Pickens District.

Issue of December 21, 1838
Married on Wednesday evening, the 21st October, by Jessee S. Magee, Esq., Mr. Stephen Baldwin to Mrs. Drusilla Grissop, all of Pickens District.
Married on the 18th October last, in Landerdale County, Mississippi, Mr. C. W. Miller Jun'r, formerly of this District, to Miss Lydia Keaton.

Issue of December 28, 1838
Married on Tuesday evening, the 18th inst., by the Rev. William Magee, Mr. Albert T. Carpenter to Miss Caroline Padgett, all of this District.
Married on Sunday evening, the 9th inst., by James Gilmer, Esc., Mr. Benjamin Carroll to Mrs. Elizabeth Goodwin, all of Anderson District.
Married on the 23d by the Pev. Wm. C. Mullinnix, Mr. Amos Morris to Elizabeth Crist, both of Anderson District.

Issue of January 4, 1839
Married at Pendleton on Thursday, the 20th December by the Rev. C. C. Pinckney, Mr. Archibald Hamilton Seabrook of Edisto Island, to Phoebe Caroline, eldest daughter of C. C. Pinckney, Fsq.
Departed this life on the evening of 11 December, Mrs. Louisa Berry, wife of Capt. Joel H. Berry, of this District. (eulogy).

Issue of January 11, 1839
Married on the 3d inst., by William Oliver, Esq., Mr. John Neal to Miss Sarah Thomas, all of Pickens District.

Issue of February 1, 1839
Married on Thursday evening, the 3d inst., bv A. O. Norris, Esq., Mr.
Tillman Tate, to Miss Cynthia, daughter of Mr. William Long, all of
Anderson District.
Married on Sunday evening, the 27th inst., bv A. O. Norris, Esq., Mr.
Blueford McDaniel, to Miss Elizabeth Hannah, all of Anderson District.
Married on the 23d inst., bv the Rev. S. Vandiver, Mr. Jas. M. Cam-
brell, to Miss Amarillis A., youngest daughter of G. Horton.

Issue of February 8, 1839
Married on the 31st January last by Rev. James Mullikin, Mr. William
S. Williams to Miss Harriet B. Worthington, both of Pickens District.
Death of Judge Charles J. Colcock, President of the Bank of the State
on Saturday night, at his residence in Broad Street (Charleston).

Issue of February 15, 1839
Married on the 7th inst., by the Rev. Wm. G. Mullinix, Mr. Obediah L.
Cann of Abbeville, to Miss Francis P. Gains, of Pickens.

Issue of March 8, 1839
Married on the 26th ult., by Rev. David Seal, Mr. Benjamin F. Holland,
to Miss Penelope, daughter of Mr. Wm. Kirksey, of Pickens District.
Another hero of the Revolution gone! Departed this life on Mondav,
the 25th ult., at his residence on Tugaloo River, Pickens District, Maj.
David Humphreys, in the 86th year of his age. He was an officer of the
Revolution. He has left numerous descendants....

Issue of March 15, 1839
Married on Thursday evening, the 28th February, by Rev. W. Magee, Mr.
Martin Smith to Miss Nancy Caroline, daughter of Mr. Jesse Magee, decd,
all of this District.
Married on Wednesday evening, the 6th inst., by Rev. S. Vandiver, Mr.
Rob't Honey, to Miss Polly, daughter of Mr. Aaron Moore, both of Pickens
District.
Departed this life at her residence in Anderson Village, on the even-
ing of the 15th of February, Mrs. Rhoda Brown, consort of Mr. Daniel
Brown, in the 36th year of her age. The deceased was the mother of nine
children...member of the Baptist Church.

Issue of March 29, 1839
Married on Wednesday evening, the 20th inst., in the Baptist Church in
Anderson Village, by the Rev'd William Magee, Mr. Robert B. Lewis to Miss
Juliet Hammond, daughter of John Hammond, all of this district.
Departed this life on Friday, the 8th inst., Mr. Joshua Hammond, in
the 68th year of his age.

Issue of April 5, 1839
Departed this life on the 12th of March last, Mr. Joshua Hammond,
aged 67 years and 4 months. He has left a widow and several children.

Issue of May 3, 1839
Married on Tuesday evening, last, by the Rev. W. T. Potter, Dr. Will-
iam L. Jenkins, to Miss Jane Gaillard, all of this District.
Married on Tuesday, the 26th March by the Rev. D. Humphreys, Mr. Peden
of Greenville, to Miss Esther Baker, of this district.
Married on the 28th of the same month, Mr. Martin Bowie to Miss Nancy
Lewis of Abbeville District.
Married on the 18th April, Mr. ___ White to Miss ___ Beaty, both of
this District.

Issue of May 17, 1839
Died at Rockfield, his residence near this village, on the 6th inst.,
in the 55th year of his age, the Hon. Samuel Prioleau...among the ablest
counsellors at the Charleston Bar....
Died in Pickens County, Alabama, on the 3d of April inst., Mrs.
Perthena Moorhead, wife of Mr. Samuel Moorhead, in the 36th year of her
age, leaving a husband & 8 small children. Columbus (Miss) Argus.

Issue of May 24, 1839
Departed this life on Monday the 13th inst., Richard Lewis Hannon, in
the 27th year of his age. He was a native of North Carolina, but lately

60

a resident of this district.

Issue of May 31, 1839
Departed this life on Saturday last, the 25th inst., James Simpson Liddell, youngest son of James S. & Jane Liddel, aged nine months.

Issue of June 7, 1839
Died at his residence near this place, on Monday morning last, Jacob Warley, Esq., clerk of the Senate of this State.
Died on the 11th ult., at Jacksonville, Al., Dr. Matthew Bart, formerly of this District.

Issue of June 21, 1839
Died at her residence in Walker Co. (Ga.), on the 26th March, Mrs. Lydia Dickson, in the 51st year of her age...member of the Presbyterian Church...left an interesting family of children...Charleston Observer.

Issue of July 5, 1839
Married on the 2d inst., by Rev. W. G. Mullinix, Mr. Charles Morris of Pickens, to Mrs. Agnes Forbes, of Anderson District.
Tribute of Respect to Dr. Hugh McCann, from physician of Greensborough, Alabama.

Issue of July 12, 1839
Died in DeKalb Co., Ga., on Monday night, June 17th, John Hays, in the 88th year of his age. Also on Wednesday evening, the 19th at 2 o'clock, Mary Hays, his wife. They emigrated from their native State, Virginia, in the autumn of 1783, to South Carolina. They resided upwards of 40 years in Pendleton District, on the waters of Pockey River. From thence they removed to Georgia, in the winter of 1826 and '7...member of the Methodist Episcopal Church for half a century or more.

Issue of July 19, 1839
Married on the 4th inst., by William Oliver, Esq., Mr. William O. Brock, to Miss Lucy Hannah Garvin, all of Pickens District.

Issue of July 26, 1839
Married on Thursday evening, the 11th inst., by the Rev. J. W. Lewis, Mr. John D. Swift to Miss Francis Knox, daughter of Mrs. Eliza Knox, both of Franklin Co., Ga.

Issue of September 6, 1839
Married on the 22d ult., by Rev. W. G. Mullinix, Mr. Edley L. Hamilton to Miss Margaret Miller, all of Pickens District.
Married at Anderson C. H., by the Rev. B. D. Dupre, on the 29th ult., Mr. Lewis Belot to Miss Amanda Richardson, all of this District.
Died at this place, on the 22d of August, Mr. John F. Lewis, in the 35th year of his age. (eulogy).

Issue of September 13, 1839
Married on the 5th inst., at the residence of Rev. David Humphreys, Dr. Thomas Lee of Abbeville, to Miss Elizabeth Lee Humphreys.
Married on last evening, by the Rev. W. G. Mullinix, Mr. James J. Duke of Pickens District, to Miss Ann R. Miller, of this village.

Issue of September 27, 1839
Died at her father's residence in this District, on the 18th inst., Jane Melissa, daughter of David and Mary Russell, aged 10 years and 6 months.

Issue of November 1, 1839
Married on Thursday evening, the 20th ult., by Rev. Wm. Magee, Mr. Isaac C. Richey to Miss Elizabeth Jane, eldest daughter of Mr. John Razor, all of Abbeville District.

Issue of November 8, 1839
Married on Thursday evening, the 24th ult., by Rev. Joseph Grisham, Mr. Jesse Garner to Miss Eliza Ann Parsons, all of Pickens District.

Issue of November 15, 1839
Married on Thursday evening the 7th inst., by Rev. Wm Magee, Mr. John
Maldin of Abbeville District, to Miss Harriet, daughter of Mr. Elijah
Wyatt of Anderson District.
Married on the 7th inst., by Rev. Wm. Mullinix, Mr. John Smith sen.,
to Elizabeth Powell, both of Anderson District.

Issue of November 22, 1839
Married on the 7th inst., by Rev. B. D. Dupre, Mr. W. C. Smith to
Miss Elizabeth M. Lewis, all of Anderson District.
Married on the 19th inst., by Rev. Wm Mullinix, Mr. Washington E.
Holcombe, to Miss Elizabeth, daughter of Dr. Jno. Robinson, all of Pickens
District.

Issue of November 29, 1839
Married on the 21st inst., by Rev. Wm Mullinix, Mr. Daniel Loving, of
Anderson District, to Miss Rebecca Melinda Hopkins, of Pickens District.

Issue of December 6, 1839
Married on Thursday evening, the 28th ult., by Rev. Wm Magee, Mr.
William A. Trussell to Miss Fanny McCoy, all of Anderson district.
Departed this life at Fair Play, S. C. on the 25th November, Edward
W., son of Rev. Sanford Vandiver, in the 21st year of his age. He has
left a father, mother, brothers and sisters.

Issue of December 20, 1839
Married on Wednesday evening last, by the Rev. Mr. Kennedy, Mr. Thomas
H. Russell, to Miss Martha Jane, daughter of Col. David K. Hamilton,
all of this District.
Married on Tuesday evening, the 10th inst., by Rev. Hiram Lecrov,
Mr. John Sanders, to Miss Louisa J. Beaty, all of Anderson District.
Married on Thursday evening, the 12th inst., by the Rev. Sanford
Vandiver, Mr. John M. Burriss to Miss Keziah Jones, all of Anderson Dist.
Married on the 17th ult., by the same, Mr. Washington Holms of
Gwinnett Co., Ga., to Miss Martha W. Havey of Anderson District.

Issue of December 27, 1839
Married on Tuesday evening last by the Rev. W. C. Mullinix, Mr. Nim-
rod T. Smith to Miss Martha Eliza Majors.
Also by the same, on the same evening, Mr. Jas L. Carpenter, to Miss
Jane S. Majors, daughters of John Majors, all of Anderson District.
Married on Wednesday evening last, by the Rev. James Hembree, Mr.
Leroy N. Rainwater to Miss Hannah, daughter of Whitaker Smith, sen.

Issue of January 10, 1840
Married on the 2d inst., by Rev. W. C. Mullinix, Mr. John G. Smith,
to Miss Amanda, daughter of James and Sarah Smith, both of Anderson
District.
Married on Thursday evening, the 26th ult., by Rev. Wm Magee, Mr.
Gabriel L. Magee to Miss Eliza, daughter of Lewis Bozeman, Esq., all of
Anderson District.
Married on Thursday evening, the 2d inst., by the same. Mr. Bartlett
Milam of Laurens District, to Miss Rachel A. Richardson, of Anderson
Village.

Issue of January 17, 1840
Died at his residence in this vicinity, on the night of the 8th inst.,
Mr. Samuel Cherry, in the 66th year of his age. Mr. Cherry was an old
and well-known inhabitant of this District, which he represented at
different times in branches of the Legislature. He was a successful
merchant of our village.
Died in Abbeville, on the 30th December, Leander Gaillard, son of
Whitfield and Sarah Holleman, aged 2 years, 2 months, and 10 days.

Issue of January 24, 1840
Married on Athens, Ga., on the 7th inst., by the Rev. Mr. Hoyt, Mr.
Benjamin F. Whitner, of Florida, to Miss Sarah Jane, daughter of Rev.
Alonzo Church, of the former place.
Married on the 6th inst., by Rev.Mr. Humphreys, Mr. Scott, to Miss
Vina Parker,all of Anderson District.

62

Married on Sunday evening, the 12th inst., by Zachariah Hall, Esq.,
Mr. Philip Cromer to Miss Sarah, daughter of Henry Cable, all of this
District.
Married on Thursday, the 16th inst., by Pev. S. Vandiver, Mr. Thomas
H. Simmons, to Miss Anna H., daughter of the late Col. John Harris.
Married on Thursday, the 16th inst., by Miles M. Norton, Esq., Mr.
William L. Wilson to Miss Mary Colhoon, all of Pickens.
Departed this life on the 30th ult., in his 25th year, Mr. Elijah A.
Belotte, at the residence of his father, Mr. Peter Belotte.

Issue of February 7, 1840
Married on Sunday evening, the 2d inst., by the Pev. W. Magee, Mr.
Samuel McCoy Junr., to Miss Amanda F. Taylor all of Anderson District.

Issue of February 21, 1840
Married on Thursday evening, the 13th inst., by the Rev. A. W. Poss,
James W. Harrison, Esq., to Miss Mary J., daughter of Mr. E. P. Penson,
of this village.
Married on Thursday evening, the 13th inst., by Rev. W. Magee, Mr.
William F. Wright, to Miss Catherine E., youngest daughter of James
Brock, Esq., all of Anderson District.
Died at Pumpkintown, S. C. on Monday evening, the 27th ult., Capt.
Amos L. Sutherland, aged 25 years & 4 months, son of Wm. and Sarah
Sutherland of that place. His death was caused by a fall from a horse....
He commanded the Pumpkintown Artillery company.

Issue of February 28, 1840
Married on the 16th inst., by J. A. Moore, Esq., Mr. Elam Holland,
to Miss Elizabeth Allen.
Married on the 20th inst., by the same, Mr. Benjamin James to Miss
C. McLewis, all of Pickens District.

Issue of March 6, 1840
Married on Thursday evening, the 21st February, by Pev. W. Magee, Mr.
William McDavid of Greenville District, to Miss Agnes C. Gilkison of
Abbeville District.
Married on the 18th February, by Rev. David Humphreys, Mr. Robert
Keys to Miss Cinderella, daughter of Mr. John E. Morris.
February 3, 1840: Died this morning at five o'clock, Mrs. Dorcas
Gray, at the house of her father, S. Cunningham, Esq., in this District.
She came from Mississippi to Carolina, on a visit to her friends in com-
pany with her children and was never able to return...(long eulogy).

Issue of March 20, 1840
Died at Anderson C. H., on Friday morning, the 12th inst., George
Washington Liddell, son of David and Mary Russell, aged 13 years and 4
months.

Issue of April 3, 1840
Married on the 5th inst., by Pev. J. L. Kennedy, Mr. Jackson Anderson
to Miss Nancy, daughter of the late Mr. Weyman Holland, all of Pickens
District.

Issue of April 17, 1840
Patrick Noble died at Abbeville, on the 7th inst., For a long series
of years, represented his district in the Legislature. In 1838, he was
chosen Governor of the State. The duties of his office will devolve on Dr.
B. K. Hennegan of Marlborough district, who is Lieutenant Governor.

Issue of April 24, 1840
Married on Thursday evening, the 9th inst., by Rev. W. M gee, Mr.
Clement L. Nelson of Abbeville District, to Miss Nancy M. Robinson of
Anderson District.

Issue of May 15, 1840
Married on Thursday evening, the 7th inst., by Rev. W. Magee, Mr. Ollev
Mattison to Miss Mary Clement, all of Anderson District.

Issue of May 29, 1840
Married on the evening of the 17th inst., by Rev. S. Vandiver, Mr.

Lewis W. Holmes to Miss Lucinda Ramsay, all of Elbert Co., Ga.

Issue of June 5, 1840

Married on Tuesday morning, the 2d inst., by Rev. A. W. Ross, Mr. John Smyth Walker, to Miss Eleanor Jane, daughter of Wm. McElmoyle of Charleston, S. C.

Died near this placeon Friday morning, the 29th ult., aged 64 years, Mr. Crosby V. Miller, one of our oldest and most respectable citizens. Mr. M. passed the greater part of his life in this vicinity...He has left a widow, and large family of children.

Issue of June 12, 1840

Died at his residence in Pickens District, on Saturday, the 6th inst., of a pulmonary disease, Mr. John C. Kilpatrick Jr., aged 31 years.

Issue of June 26, 1840

Married on the 16th inst., by Stephen Reid, Esq., Mr. William Kirksey, jr., to Miss Catharine, daughter of J. R. Reid, all of Pickens District.

Issue of July 3, 1840

Married on Monday evening, the 11th ult., by James Gilmer Esq., Mr. John W. Vickory, to Miss Clarissa White, all of Anderson District.

Issue of July 10, 1840

Married on the 5th inst., by Rev. W. G. Mullinix, Mr. Thomas Alexander to Miss Mary, daughter of N. Boon, Esq., all of Pickens District.

Issue of July 24, 1840

Death of Hon. Jas. R. Pringle...(at Charleston) on Friday evening last...President of State Senate, 1819, appointed collector of Customs by President James Monroe...interred in St. Michael's Churchyard.... Char. Cour.

Issue of July 31, 1840

Major William Milwee of Anderson district, departed this life, 15th of July, 4 minutes after 12 o'clock PM, aged 88 years. He was a citizen of S. C. at the commencement of the Revolution, and a true friend to the cause of liberty.

Issue of August 15, 1840

Married on the evening of the 7th inst., by Wm. D. Steele, Esq., Mr. James Cosset to Miss Delila Wright, all of Pickens District.

Married on Wednesday the 5th inst., by Wm. McMurry, Esq., Mr. Ezekiel Pilgrim to Miss Sarah B. Bates, all of Pickens District.

Issue of August 21, 1840

Married on Thursday, the 3d inst., by Rev. W. Magee, Mr. P. McPhail to Miss Malvina H., daughter of Mrs. Mary L. Richardson, all of Anderson Village.

Married on Monday evening, the 17th ult., by the Rev. H. Wood, Mr. U. C. Roe to Miss Malinda, daughter of James Holden all of Pickens District.

Issue of August 28, 1840

Death of Rev. Charles W. Martin. Departed this life on Monday, the 17th inst., at the residence of his father in Abbeville District, in the 29th year of his age. He left an aged father & mother, 2 infant children, and brothers and sisters. He had in view the profession of law, but whilst in College in Danville, Ky., he attached himself to the Presbyterian Church...at the age of 21, completed his course in Miami University, Oxford, Ohio, and returned to S. C. He married in 1833, and five years afterwards experienced a severe trial in the death of his spouse...He was ordained in 1834 (eulogy).

Died on the morning of the 24th inst., Patrick Noble, infant son of M. T. and Lucinda Miller, aged 2 months, 2 weeks, and 3 days.

Issue of September 4, 1840

Married on Tuesday evening, the 1st inst., by Rev. Mr. Kennedy, Mr. Samuel Chamblin of Spartanburgh, to Miss Jane, daughter of Mr. Thos. C. Boggs, of Pickens District.

Married on Thursday evening, the 27th inst., by Rev. Wm. Magee, Robert Shirley, Esq., to Miss Elizabeth Posey, all of Anderson District.

Married on Thursday evening, the 20th ult., by John A. Moore, Esq., Mr. John Sanders to Miss Mahalia Moore, all of Pickens District.

Departed this life on Wednesday, the 12th ult., in Creenville District, S. C., Mr. Baily Fricks, in the 28th year of his age. He has left a father, 3 sisters, and many relatives.

Issue of September 25, 1840

Married on the 17th inst., on Cane Creek, by the Rev. Mr. Dawson, Dr. R. D. Maxwell of Pendleton to Miss Lucy C. Sloan, of Pickens District.

Married on the 7th ultimo, by the Rev. B. D. Dupre, Mr. Richard H. Lee to Miss Letitia Smith, all of this District.

Married on Thursday, the 10th inst., by the Rev. James Wilson, Col. John W. Guyton to Miss Susan Wellborn, all of Anderson District.

Issue of October 9, 1840

Married on Tuesday evening, the 6th inst., by Rev. A. Rice, Mr. James Zachary of North Carolina, to Miss Eliza Ann, eldest daughter of David Russel, of Anderson District.

Departed this life on the 28th ult., in Abbeville District, Joseph W. Holleman, planter, (eulogy).

Issue of October 16, 1840

Married on Thursday evening, the 8th inst., by Rev. W. Magee, Mr. William N. Fant to Miss Mary A. Burriss, all of this District.

Issue of October 23, 1840

Departed this life on the 18th ult., in the 88th year of her age, Mrs. Agnes Anderson. She was born and raised in Virginia, Augusta County, but emigrated to this District about 55 years ago, where she has lived ever since.

Also on the 12th inst., Miss Sarah Ann Matthews, granddaughter of the above deceased, in the 20th year of her age.

Issue of October 30, 1840

Married on Thursday morning, the 29th inst., by the Rev. A. W. Ross, Capt. J. A. Evatt of Pickens District, to Miss Susan Symmes, of Anderson.

Issue of November 6, 1840

Married on Thursday evening, the 29th October last, by Rev. Stephen Powell, Mr. Zachariah Gibson to Miss Eliza B. McKinney, daughter of James McKinney, all of Pickens District.

Married on Tuesday evening, the 3rd inst., by Wm. L. Keith, Esq., Mr. George W. Banks to Miss Matilda, daughter of George Wigginton, all of Pickens District.

Issue of November 13, 1840

Married on Thursday, the 5th inst., by Miles M. Norton, Esq., Mr. Allen S. Strawhorn of Aberdeen, Miss., to Miss Nancy E., daughter of Mrs. M. Telford of Pickens District.

Issue of November 20, 1840

Married on the 17th ult., by Rev. B. D. Dupre, Mr. F. H. Tillinghast to Miss Caroline Belotte, all of this District.

Issue of November 27, 1840

Married on Tuesday evening, the 17th inst., by Rev. W. Magee, Mr. Samuel W. Williford of Anderson District, S. C. to Miss Sarah, daughter of William McMullin, Esq., of Elbert Co., Ga.

Married on the evening of the 17th inst., by Rev. A. Rice, Gen. James M. Tate of Desoto Co., Miss., to Mrs. Nancy T. Tilman of Abbeville District, S. C.

Married on Sunday the 1st inst., by Miles M. Norton, Esq., Mr. Daniel Hughes to Miss Martha Barker, all of Pickens District.

Issue of December 4, 1840

Married on Thursday evening, the 19th ult., by Rev. Wm. Magee, Mr. Marcus Motes of Laurens District to Miss Elizabeth L., eldest daughter of Mr. Moses Dean of Anderson District.

Married on Thursday, the 26th ult., by Rev. Wm. Magee, Mr. Nimrod
Crear to Miss Martha Amanda Massey, both of this District.
Died in Pickens District, S. C., Nov. 24th 1840, Mrs. Nancy D. Powers,
wife of Zechariah Powers, in the 31st year of her age...joined the Methodist Episcopal Church while she was young...She left a husband and three
small children (long eulogy).

Issue of December 18, 1840

Married on Thursday evening, the 3d inst., by the Rev. Wm. H. Barr,
Mr. H. T. Miller, to Miss Amanda, second daughter of Mr. John L. Ellis,
all of Abbeville District.
Married on Thursday evening, the 3d inst., by W. L. Keith, Esq., Mr.
Wyatt Hudson to Miss Sarah Brown, both of Pickens District.
Married on Thursday evening, the 10th inst., by the same, Mr. John
Whitmire, to Miss Nancy Stewart, both of Pickens District.

Issue of January 1, 1841

Married on Thursday evening, the 3rd ult., by the Rev. Thos Folland,
Mr. Robert D. McCroskey of Clarksville, Ga., to Miss Emeline Holland, of
Pickens District, S. C.
Married on the 17th ult., by Rev. Mr. Mullinix, Mr. Neely V. Elrod
of Anderson to Miss Harriet Williams of Pickens District.
Married on the 24th ult., by the same, Mr. Jesse H. Ellis to Miss
Judith M. Carey, all of Pickens District.
Married on the 22d ult., by Rev. D. Humphreys, Mr. Archibald Skelton
to Miss Mary Williford.
Married on the 24th ult., by the same, Dr. A. F. Thompson to Miss
Jane Norris, all of Anderson District.
Died on the 16th December past. at his residence in this District,
Capt. Lewis Shirrill, in the 80th year of his age. On the day of his
death, Mrs. Mary Shirrill, consort of the above, was taken sick and died
on the Tuesday following...members of the Baptist Church.

Issue of January 8, 1841

Married on the 24th ult., by Rev. D. Humphreys, Mr. John McMahon to
Miss ____ Moshat, all of Anderson District.

Issue of January 15, 1841

Married on Tuesday evening, the 12th inst., on Cane Creek, by the Rev.
W. G. Mullinix, Mr. A. F. Lewis to Miss Susan A. Sloan, both of Pickens
District.
Married on Wednesday evening, the 6th inst., Mr. Samuel E. Maxwell,
of Pendleton, to Miss Julia S. Kerls of Sumter, S. C.

Issue of January 22, 1841

Married on the 12th inst., by Rev. S. Vandiver, Mr. Fountain G. Moss,
of Habersham (County, Georgia), to Miss Catharine Grant, of this district.

Issue of February 5, 1841

Married on the 19th inst., by Rev. H. Tyler of Ga., Mr. John Hall of
Pickens District, to Miss Mary H. Harris of Anderson District.
Married on February 2, 1841, by Rev. B. D. Dupre, Mr. John Rothlander
to Miss Melissa McCreary, all of this District.
Married on the 14th ult., by the Rev. D. Humphreys, Mr. George Steph-
enson to Miss Sarah Dean.
Married on Thursday the 21st ult., by the Rev. Thomas Dawson, Mr.
William B. Barton to Miss Frances Lewis, both of this District.
Married on Tuesday evening, the 12th inst., by Rev. J. L. Kennedy,
Capt. A. Alexander to Miss Caroline, daughter of Capt. Jas. H. Dendy.
Married on the same evening, by Rev. Andrew McGuffin, Mr. George
Vinzant to Miss Catharine Hull, all of Pickens District.
Married on Sunday, the 31st ult., by Miles M. Norton, Esq., Mr.
Harvey Capehart to Miss Jane Golden, all of Pickens District.
Died on Monday, the 25th January, Mr. William Walker, aged about 77....
for 35 years a resident of this district...left a widow and children.
Charleston Observer, please copy.

Issue of February 12, 1841

Married on the 4th inst., by Rev. Sandford Vandiver, Mr. James P.
Gray of Abbeville, to Miss Mary Ann Frances, eldest daughter of Col John
McFall, all of Anderson District.

Married on the 7th inst., by James A. Evatt, Esq., Mr. Zachariah
Power to Miss Ruth Chapman, both of Pickens District.
Married on the 28th January, by the Rev. Thomas Dawson, Mr. Ivory
Howard to Miss Ann Lewis, both of Pickens District.

Issue of March 5, 1841
Married on Tuesday evening, the 2d inst., by Pev. W. G. Mullinix, Mr.
James Russell to Miss Malinda Lanear, all of Pickens District.

Issue of March 12, 1841
Married on the evening of the 28th ult., by William D. Steele, Esq.,
Mr. Joseph Fricks to Miss Rebecca Ivester, all of Pickens District.
Married on Sunday evening, the 28th ult., by W. Magee, Mr. Caleb B.
Holland to Miss Elizabeth Cox, all of Anderson District.
Married by the same, on Wednesday evening, the 3d March, Mr. Andrew
J. Wakefield of Abbeville District, to Miss Emeline Elizabeth McGee, of
Anderson District.

Issue of March 26, 1841
Married on Sunday evening, the 21st inst., by James Emerson, Esq., Mr.
Mr. William Shaw of Abbeville, to Miss Nancy Saylor of Anderson District.
Married on Thursday evening, the 18th inst., by Pev. Wm. Magee, Mr.
Thomas W. Davis to Miss Sarah Kay, all of this District.
Departed this life at his residence in Pickens District, on the even-
ing of the 17th inst., at 11 o'clock, Maj. James McKinney, in the 78th
year of his age. He was among the first that settled this section of the
country, and was active in securing quiet and safety to our frontiers,
from the relentless savage...(eulogy).

Issue of April 2, 1841
Married on Tuesday evening, the 30th ult., by W. L. Keith, Esq., Mr.
Sidney McDow, to Miss Margaret Craig, all of Pickens District.

Issue of April 9, 1841
Married on the 7th inst., by Rev. W. G. Mullinix, Mr. Allen Mauldin
to Miss Edaline Edama.
Died on the 4th inst., at her residence near this place, Mrs. Elizabeth Carne, consort of the late Thos. W. Carne, aged 72 years and 15 days.
...left four children...member of the Church for nearly 40 years...(eulogy).

Issue of April 16, 1841
Married on Sunday morning, the 11th inst., by Rev. David Simmons, Mr.
Robert A. Hubbard to Miss Lucinda Smith, both of Andersonville, S. C.

Issue of April 30, 1841
Married on Sunday evening, the 18th inst., by Rev. W. Magee, Mr. Henry
Mattox to Miss Matilda M. Braswell, both of this District.
Married on Sunday evening, the 25th inst., by Rev. S. Vandiver, Mr.
William Simpson to Miss Rutha Caroline Austen, all of Greenville District.

Issue of May 28, 1841
A Funeral Sermon, on the death of Mrs. Wesley Gassaway, will be
preached at Mount Zion, on the 2d Sunday in June, by Rev. Levi Garrison.

Issue of June 25, 1841
Married on Thursday evening, the 10th inst., by Fsquire Moseley, Mr.
Wm. Stewart to Miss Eliza Jenkins.

Issue of July 2, 1841
Married on the 24th ult., by Rev. S. Vandiver, Mr. William Goldsmith
of Hamburg, to Miss Mary Louisa, daughter of Capt. Banister Stone, of
Greenville District.

Issue of July 9, 1841
Married on the 4th inst., by Rev. W. G. Mullinix, Mr. Elias Odell to
Miss Elizabeth Clayton, all of Pickens District.

Issue of July 16, 1841
Another Revolutionary Patriot Gone! Died at his residence in this
District, on Wednesday morning, the 30th June, Aaron Guyton, aged 80

years. The deceased was a native of Maryland, whence his father removed to Union District, previous to the revolutionary war. He, with his elder brothers, was almost continually in the company of Sumpter or Pickens... (list of battles served in)...About 45 years ago, Mr. Guyton moved to this District, and settled on the plantation on which he died. He shortly afterward joined the Baptist Church.

Issue of August 6, 1841

Married on the 15th inst., by Wm. C. Lee, Esq., John W. Gassaway, to Miss Candis Cane, all of Pickens District.

Married on the 30th ult., by Rev. W. G. Mullinix, Mr. Matthew Mullinix to the widow Emily Whitefield, all of Pickens District.

Another Revolutionary Patriot Gone! Departed this life on Thursday, the 8th inst., at his residence in Pickens District, near Fair Play, Capt. William Guest, in the 79th year of his age, leaving a widow, sons and daughters. (eulogy).

Issue of August 20, 1841

Died in Pickens District, on the 5th August, James Gaines, Esq., aged about 58 years and 15 days. Father Gaines was born in Virginia, and was bro't to South Carolina when he was small, 30 or 35 miles from the capital of the State. He afterwards removed to Abbeville District, thence to Pickens, where he spent the last 20 years of his life. For a number of years, he was an acting magistrate of the District of Pickens, and a steady member of the Methodist Episcopal Church...He has left a wife and 10 children.

Issue of September 3, 1841

Married on Thursday evening, the 24th inst., by Rev. W. G. Mullinix, Mr. Jeptha Lay to Miss Mary C. Holland, all of Pickens District.

Married by the same, on Saturday evening, the 21st ult., Mr. George Barrett to Miss Edala Hopkins.

Died on the 25th ult., at his place of residence in this District, Mr. James Warnock, in the 67th year of his age. He has left a wife, one daughter in this and one daughter and two sons in distant places....

Issue of September 17, 1841

Departed this life, Dr. John Robinson, of Pendleton Village, in the 49th year of his age, on the 4th inst....leaves companion and 10 children. (eulogy).

Died on the night of the 7th inst., Mrs. Frances Broyles, consort of Maj. Aaron Broyles, of this District, aged near 72 years. She has left a husband and a long train of relatives and friends.

Issue of September 24, 1841

Married on Thursday evening, the 16th inst., by Rev.. W. G. Mullinix, Mr. John F. Miller of Alabama, to Miss Malinda, daughter of Mr. John Davis, of Pickens District.

Issue of October 1, 1841

From the Perry (Ala.) Eagle. Died on the 7th September, Col. William E. Blassingame. He was in the 43d year of his age, a native of Greenville District, but for the last 7 years, a citizen of Perry Co., Ala....representated his native district in the Legislature and after his emigration hither, was elected a member of the Legislature of Alabama, for this county....He has left a wife and six children...(eulogy).

Issue of October 8, 1841

Married on Wednesday evening, the 6th inst., by Rev. A. W. Ross, Mr. Alfred Fuller of this Village, to Miss Eliza Walker, of Pickens District.

Married on Tuesday the 21st ult., by Rev. W. G. Mullinix, Mr. John P. Sitton to Miss Nancy M. Wilson, all of Anderson District.

Married on Thursday, the 23d ult., by the same, Mr. J. A. Boggs, to Miss Marinda Jane Gaines, all of Pickens District.

Issue of October 15, 1841

Married on Thursday evening, Aug. 19th by the Hon. Henry F. Scruggs, William H. Jemison, Esq., to Miss Harriet P. Verner, all of Sumter Co., Alabama.

Issue of October 22, 1841
    Married on Tuesday evening, Sept. 28th, by Rev. A. Rice, Mr. Quinton
Loveless, of Cobb Co., Ga., to Miss Eliza Ann, daughter of the Widow
Hanks, of this District.
    Married on Tuesday evening, Oct. 12, by the same, Mr. Abner H., son
of Rev. W. Magee, to Miss Anna Melvina, daughter of Z. Hall, all of Anderson District.

Issue of October 29, 1841
    Married on Tuesday the 12th inst., by Rev. A. W. Poss, Barnett H.
Allgood, Esq., of Pickens District, to Miss Elizabeth Edmonston, of
Anderson District.
    Departed this life on the 13th inst., at her residence in Pickens
District, Mrs. Mary Duff, aged 67, 5 months and a few days. She was left
a widow with a large family of children (eulogy).

Issue of November 5, 1841
    Died on Friday the 8th October last at her residence near this place,
Mrs. Sarah Lewis, relict of Col. Richard Lewis, decd, aged 72 years. The
deceased was a daughter of Capt. James Miller of Rutherford Co., N. C.,
who commanded a volunteer company in the siege of Augusta, and was severe-
ly wounded in the attack. For 40 years, a member of the Methodist Episcopal Church.

Issue of November 12, 1841
    Married on Sunday evening last, by Rev. W. C. Mullinix, Mr. T. J.
Werner, to Miss Frances E. Ambers, all of this District.
    Died in the neighborhood of Pendleton, on the 25th October, Rev. Jas-
per Adams, D. D., in the 48th year of his age. He was first tutor and
then Professor of Mathematics of Brown University; then President of
Charleston College; also of Geneva College in New York; afterward Chaplain
and Professor of Moral Philosophy at West Point. (eulogy).

Issue of November 19, 1841
    Married on Sunday evening, the 7th inst., by James Mullikin, Esq., Mr.
Andrew Owen to Miss Jane Brewer, of this District.

Issue of November 26, 1841
    Married on Thursday evening, the 18th inst., by Rev. A. Rice, Mr.
James Drake to Miss Malinda Jane, eldest daughter of James Emerson, Esq.

Issue of December 3, 1841
    Died at his residence near the village of Pendleton, S. C., on the
30th November, Col. Samuel Warren, in the 81st year of his age, one of
our revolutionary worthies. He lost a leg at the attack on Savannah. He
served in both branches of the Legislature, and was President of the Senate.

Issue of December 10, 1841
    Died on the 3d inst., at the House of Thos. Dawson, Jenkin S. Jenkins,
a native of Wales, and for the last 44 years a citizen of this county
(sic); he was for many years pastor of a Welch church in Philadelphia, and
moved at S. C. about 12 years ago.

Issue of December 17, 1841
    Died in this District, on the 1st inst., Mrs. Elizabeth McElmoyle, aged
66, late of Charleston...left a husband and several daughters.
    Died in Pickens District, on the 30th November, Jesse Stribling, Esq.,
an old and respectable citizen.
    Died near Hickstown, Florida, on the 14th ult., William H. Harrison,
Esq., a native, and until the last year, a resident of this district. He
was a young man of great moral worth.
    Tribute of Respect to William Henry Harrison by Anderson Troop of
Cavalry.

Issue of December 24, 1841
    Married in Polk Co., Tenn., on Tues, 30th November ult., Mr. Euclid
Waterhouse of Cleveland, Tenn., to Miss Cornelia F., daughter of Capt.
John Townes of Polk Co., Tenn.

Married on November 21, by the Rev. W. C. Mullinix, Mr. D. D. Pite, to Mrs. E. A. Waters, all of Pickens District.

Married on December 14, by the same, Mr. Lemuel Thomas, to Mrs. Sarah Alexander, all of Pickens District.

Died on the 1st inst., at Double Branches, Anderson District, Mrs. Elizabeth, wife of William McElmoyle, Esq. She was a native of Londonderry, Ireland, where she united with the Presbyterian Church. She emigrated to this county(sic) more than 40 years ago; was married in Philadelphia, and removed with her husband to this city in 1802, where she joined the First Presbyterian Church, and on the organization of the second Presbyterian Church, she became one of its members...Her four daughters living and her husband are all members of the same church... Char. Observer, 11th inst.

Issue of December 10, 1841
Died in the village of Anderson, on Wednesday, the 8th inst., Mrs. Caroline Webb, wife of Elijah Webb, Esq., in the 34th year of her age... member of the Baptist Church. (eulogy).

Issue of January 21, 1842
Married on the 21st December ult., by the Rev. W. C. Mullinix, Mr. Joshua Owens to Miss Caroline Watson, both of Anderson District.

Died on the 5th inst., in Pickens District, Capt. James A. Evatt... (eulogy)...cut off in the flower of his days.

Died on the 11th inst., Mr. James Carvin, aged about 71, one of the first settlers of this District.

Issue of January 28, 1842
Married on the 13th inst., by Rev. Henry Tyer of Georgia, Mr. Jarard Howard to Miss Eliza Cosper, daughter of Rev. Jacob Cosper of Anderson District, S. C.

Issue of February 11, 1842
Married on Thursday evening, the 27th ult., by the Rev. W. P. Arnold, Wm. M. McIntosh, Esq., of Elberton, Ga., to Miss M. L. Allen, of Elbert Co., Ga.

Married on the same evening, by the same, Mr. Henry J. Sanders of Anderson District, to Miss Sarah H. H. Tucker, of Elbert Co., Ga.

Issue of February 18, 1842
Another of the Patriot Band Gone. Died on Thursday, the 11th inst., at his residence in Pickens District, Mr. John Craig, at the age of about 81. Mr. Craig was a soldier of the Revolution...then a resident of York or Chester district, but for the last half century, he has lived in Pendleton.

Issue of February 25, 1842
Married at West Union, S. C. on the 9th inst., by the Rev. Joseph Grisham, Wade Hampton Nations of Pickens District, S. C. to Miss Mary Ann Trammel of Henderson Co., N. C.

Married at West Union S, C. on the 15th inst., by the Rev. Joseph Grisham, Mr. Jesse Trammel of Henderson Co., N. C. to Miss Margaret Maria Natios (sic), of Pickens District, S. C.

Died on the 10th inst., at his residence near Pickens C. H., John Craig, in the 82 year of his age...one of the venerable Patriots of the Revolution. In early life he left Ireland with his father for Carolina, who settled in Chester District.

Died near Sandy Spring Camp Ground, on the 13th inst., Mary Rebecca Miller, daughter of Mathew T. and Lucinda Miller, in the 13th year of her age. (eulogy).

Issue of March 11, 1842
Married on the 1st March 1842, by Rev. D. Humphreys, Rev. Wm. P. Harris of Abbeville District, to Miss Henrietta Anderson of Spartanburg.

Issue of April 15, 1842
Married on the 8th March, by Rev. David Humphreys, Mr. Thomas Cook to Miss Malinda Moshet, all of Anderson District.

Married on the 31st March, by the same, Mr. John A. McBride to Miss Jane Haslet, of Abbeville.

Issue of May 6, 1842
Died on the 23d inst., in Pickens District, Mrs. Hannah Barton, wife of William Barton, esq., in the 62d year of her age, of cancer in her breast...left no children...(eulogy).

Issue of May 27, 1842
Died near Pendleton Village, on the 19th inst., Mrs. Dinah Winter, aged about 64. She was a native of England, and emigrated to America in the year 1816. At an early age, she embraced religion among the Episco-pal Methodists.

Issue of July 1, 1842
Married on the 10th of May last, by Rev. Richard Phillips, Doct. Major J. Lewis of Cumming, Forsyth Co., Ga., formerly of Pock Mills, S. C., to Miss Evelina Jane, daughter of Mr. Thomas Lenoir of Gwinnett Co., Ga.
Departed this life on the 30th May, in Lauderdale Co., Ala., Mary Elizabeth Thompson, aged 34 years, 5 months and 7 days, wife of Joseph Thompson, and daughter of Samuel Maverick of this place. She left a husband, five children, a father, brother and sister.

Issue of August 26, 1842
Died on the 12th inst., Mrs. Susan Evatt. Seven months since she was left a widow, and now leaves an infant son, too young to feel the loss he has sustained.
Died on the 17th, Mrs. Jane Bishop, wife of Mr. Nicholas Bishop, in the 84th year of her age. She was the daughter of Maj. Michael Dickson, who was an officer in the Revolution....member of the Presbyterian Church ...She has left an aged husband, and a number of descendants.
Died on the 10th inst., near Edgefield C. H., Eldred Simkins, only son of Hon. Francis W. Pickens, aged about 3 years, and on the 12th his mother, Mrs. Margaret Eliza, wife of Hon. Mr. Pickens.

Issue of September 23, 1842
Married on the 24th ult., by the Rev. William T. Hamilton, Malcom J. McRea, Esq., to Miss Mary Ann, daughter of Gen. Wm. Taylor of this city. MobileRegister.
Married on last evening, by Rev. W. G. Mullinix, Maj. Willis Robinson of Pickensville to Miss Sarah Ann, daughter of J. C. Griffin, Esq., of Anderson District.
Mrs. Letitia Tyler, wife of the President of the U. S., expired at 8 o'clock on the evening of Saturday last....
Died recently near Hamburg, S. C., Col. Samuel Hammond, in the 87th year of his age, an officer of the Revolution.
Died in Walker Co., Ga., Rev. Wm. McQuillen of the Presbyterian Church.

Issue of September 30, 1842
Died September 25, at the Glen (near Pendleton Village), Catharine Amarinthea Percy, infant daughter of Dr. Arthur S. Gibbes, aged 14 months and 2 days.

Issue of October 21, 1842
Married on the 15th September by Rev. Wm. Magee, Mr. Samuel Dean of Mississippi, to Miss Mary H., daughter of Mr. Moses Dean of Anderson District.

Issue of October 28, 1842
Married on Thursday evening, the 13th inst., by Rev. J. L. Kennedy, Mr. C. M. Lay to Miss Elizabeth Boggs, daughter of Wm. Boggs, all of Pickens District.

Issue of November 18, 1842
Married on the 8th inst., by Rev. Wm. G. Mullinnex, of Pickens, Mr. James Young of Abbeville to Miss Mary Elizabeth Clayton of Pickens.
Married on the morning of the 8th inst., at 12 o'clock, in New York, Dr. Van Buren of U. S. N., son of the Ex-President, led to the altar the accomplished eldest daughter of the celebrated Dr. Mott of New York. Char. Pat.

Issue of December 16, 1842
    Married on the 6th inst., by Rev. Mr. Landrum, Maj. ____ Bomar of
Spartanburgh to Mrs. Sarrah Blassengame of this place.
    Married on the 8th inst., by Rev. Andrew Mcguffin, Mr. Nimrod Emery
to Miss Elizabeth M. Magee, of Pickens District.
    Married on the 8th inst., by Rev. B. D. DuPre, Mr. John E. Belotte,
to Miss Susana Catharine DuPre, of Anderson District.

Issue of January 13, 1843
    Married on the evening of the 25th ultimo, by Elijah Alexander, Esq.,
Mr. Robert O. Wigington, to Miss Mary Liddleton, all of Pickens District.
    Married on the evening of the 29th ultimo, by Elijah Alexander, Esq.,
Mr. Arthur Wilson to Miss Milly Liddleton, all of Pickens District.
    Married on the 11th inst., at Pendleton Factory, by Rev. Joseph
Grisham, Mr. D. H. Harris to Miss Margaret Welch.
    Married on Tuesday the 5th inst., by Rev. Wm. G. Mullinix, Henry C.
Boggs, to Miss Caroline Mason, all of Pickens District.
    Married on Sunday, the 8th inst., by Rev. Wm. G. Mullinix, Riley J.
Richey, to Miss Malissa Hood, all of Pickens District.
    Married on Tuesday the 10th inst., by Rev. Wm. G. Mullinix, Ellis
Hopkins of Pendleton to Miss Mary Ann Rebecca Christian of Pendleton.

Issue of January 20, 1843
    Married on the 10th instant by E. Alexander, Esq., Mr. Joseph Golden
to Miss Elizabeth, eldest daughter of Mr. William Wilson, all of Pickens
District.
    Died on Friday last in Pickens District, in the 73d year of his age,
Mr. George Grace, formerly of Greenville. He leaves a widow, with whom
he had lived in wedlock more than half a century.

Issue of January 27, 1843
    Married on the 19th inst., by Rev. W. G. Mullinix, Rev. G. W. Barnes
of Abbeville to Miss Arabella A. R. Dart of this place.
    Died on the 9th inst., at her son's residence in Pickens District,
Mrs. Jane Hamilton...in the 84th year of her age...member of Presbyterian
Church...son Thomas...(eulogy).

Issue of February 3, 1843
    Died on Monday, 30th January, at his father's residence near Pendle-
ton, Zachariah T. Broyles, aged 15 years.

Issue of February 10, 1843
    Married on the 2d inst., by Rev. W. G. Mullinix, Mr. Samuel Newton of
Anderson to Miss Elizabeth Parks of Pickens.
    Married on the 7th inst., by E. Alexander, Esq., Mr. James A. White
to Miss Lei Wigington, all of Pickens District.

Issue of February 17, 1843
    Married on the 9th of February, in Hamburg, by David C. Taylor, Esq.,
Mr. Wm. Myer of Hamburg, to Miss Louisa Swords of Anderson District.
    Married on Wednesday evening, the 8th inst., by Rev. A. Rice, Mr.
John R. Towns, to Miss Ann Melvina, daughter of Rev. William Magee, all
of this District.

Issue of February 24, 1843
    Married on the 5th inst., by A. Rodd, Esq., Mr. George Brown to Miss
Susannah Latham, both of Anderson.
    Married on Wednesday evening, the 8th inst., by Rev. A. Rice, Mr.
John R. Towers to Miss Ann Melvina, daughter of Rev. William Magee.
(notice similiar announcement in last issue--BHH).

Issue of March 31, 1843
    Married on the 19th inst., by Rev. William G. Mullinix, of Pickens,
Mr. Stephen Gitrey of Anderson to Miss Elizabeth Hopkins, of Pickens
District.
    Death of Dr. Edward W. North Sr., formerly mayor of our city....
Charleston Mercury.
    Died on the 22d inst., at his residence in Greenville District, Maj.
Thomas Benson, in the 82d year of his age...a native of Virginia, where
he entered the service of the Revolution till its close. He then removed

to S. C. For 8 years, he represented Greenville in the Senate. He has
left a numerous family.
Died at her residence near Calhoun on the 23d February ult., Mrs.
Edney Brown, wife of Dr. G. R. Brown, in the 43d year of her age...member
of the Baptist Church...left a husband and seven children.

Issue of April 7, 1843
Died on the 21st ult., Miss Margaret, daughter of James C. Griffin,
Esq., And on the 30th, James C. Griffin, Esq., in the 74 years of his
age, having resided on the place where he died more than half a century.
Departed this life on the 14th of March, Mrs. Ann DuPre Gaillard,
consort of Dr. C. L. Gaillard, aged 28 years, 8 months, and 10 days...
left a husband and five small children.

Issue of April 14, 1843
Married on Wednesday evening, the 5th inst., by Rev. C. C. Pinckney,
Lionel H. Kennedy, M. D. of Spartanburgh, to Helen F., eldest daughter
of the late Lieut. C. W. Stevens, of U. S. N.
Departed this life at half past 4 o'clock this morning, at the resi-
dence of J. C. Anderson, Mr. LeRoy Warnock, a citizen of this place,
a native of S. C., from whence he emigrated to this place about 1831.
Liberty (Mississippi) Advocate.

Issue of May 5, 1843
Married in Wilkes Co., N. C. on the 13th inst., Chang-Eng, the cele-
brated Siamses Twins, to MissAdelaide Sarah, daughter of David Yates,
Esq. Yorkville Compiler.
Died on the 12th April 1843, in Dahlonega, Lumpkin Co., Ga., Robert
Emile, eldest and only surviving child of Mr. Robert B. Lewis, aged 3
years and 27 days.

Issue of May 19, 1843
Married on the 11th inst., by Rev. _ C. Mullinix, Mr. Marshall D.
Stricklin, to Miss Nancy C. Adams, all of Pickens District.
Married by the same, on the 4th inst., Mr. P. J. Miller of Pickens
to Miss Sarah J. Miller, of Anderson.
Died in this place on the morning of the 18th instant, in the 26th
year of his age, John C. Ackley, a native of Hartford, Connecticut, but
for the last four years, a resident of Rochester, N. Y.

Issue of June 23, 1843
Married in this village, on Wednesday evenin last, by the Rev. Mr.
Ross, Mr. John S. Lorton to Mrs. Eliza Amanda Kilpatrick.

Issue of July 7, 1843
Died at the Martin Springs, Spartanburgh District, S. C., on the 31st
of May, Mr. Marcus Motes, in the 34th year of his age. The deceased was
born and raised in Laurens District, S. C., and for a short period, resident and merchant of Anderson Village. In November 1840 he married
Miss Elizabeth L., eldest daughter of Mr. Moses Dean. In the spring of
'42 he visited some relations in the upper part of Georgia and Alabama.
Died in Laurens District, on the 13th June, Sarah Narcissa, only
child of Mr. Marcus and Elizabeth L. Motes, aged 5 months and 11 days.

Issue of August 11, 1843
Married on Sunday, the 6th inst., by Miles M. Norton, Esq., Mr. John
Marshall Youngblood, to Miss Rebecca, daughter of Mr. William Capehart,
all of Pickens District.

Issue of October 20, 1843
Married in Pickens District, on the 5th inst., by Wm C. Lee, Esq.,
Mr. William Meridith, to Miss Sarah, daughter of Mr. Allen Burnes.
Married on the same evening, by the same, Mr. Wyatt Garner, to Miss
Peggy Ann, daughter of Mr. Daniel Fullerton.

Issue of October 27, 1843
Married on the 19th inst., at Anderson Village, by Rev. Wm. C. Mul-
linnix, Maj. Barnet S. Gaines to Miss Margaret G., daughter of J. T.
Whitefield, Esq.

Died on the evening of the 17th inst., at the residence of his father, Mr. James Harrison at Andersonville, Dr. Elias Harrison, a young man of unsullied character.

Issue of November 24, 1843
    Died at Saturday evening,at his residence near this place, Mr. Nicholas Bishop, aged 83 years. He was, in early life, actively engaged in our Revolutionary struggle, and in several battles fought on the borders of this state and North Carolina, in one of which he had a brother killed. For nearly half a century, a resident of this district.
    Died in Henry Co., Ga., on the 30th of October, Mrs. Maria Dench, wife of John C. Dench, formerly of this place. She was a native of England...member of the Presbyterian Church.
    Died on the 7th inst., at the residence of his son in Columbia, Joseph Black, Esq., another revolutionary soldier, aged 80 years, 9 months, and 20 days. He was well known throughout the state, having represented Abbeville District in the Legislature for about 30 years. He retired from Public Life in 1840.
    Died in Abbeville District, on the 14th inst., Mr. John Archer, aged about 58, formerly of this place.
    Died at the house of John Abbett, on the North fork of Conneross, Pickens District, on the 14th inst., Mary Abbett, aged 72 years on 22 October last. She left an aged husband, and numerous relatives.

Issue of December 1, 1843
    Died on Saturday afternoon, the 25th inst., Mr. Jacob W. Warley, aged 24, a widowed mother is deprived of an affectionate son.

Issue of December 8, 1843
    Died in Pickens District, on the morning, of the 22d ult., Mrs. Clarissa Kilpatrick, wife of Col. John C. Kilpatrick, aged 72 years.
    And on Tuesday morning, the 5th inst., Col. John C. Kilpatrick. If he had lived till the 29th of the present month, he would have completed his 80th year. Col. Kilpatrick was one of the first settlers in this part of the country, having emigrated when quite a young man from the borders of North Carolina, where we believe he was born. He was present at the treaty of Hopewell, held near this place in 1785, with the Cherokee, Creek, Choctaw and Chickasaw tribes.
    Departed this life on the 28th November, Mrs. Martha Humphreys, aged 73 years. (eulogy).

Issue of January 19, 1844
    Died of Idiopathic Croup on ____ inst., Frederick Broyles, 3rd ____ ____ jah Estes, just entered his 5th year, the 8th February last,____ Thomas, 4th son, aged 18 months   . (torn).
    Married on Sunday evening, the 14th inst., by Elijah Alexander, Mr. Berry Wilson to Miss Charity White, all of Pickens District.

Issue of January 26, 1844
    Married on the evening, of the 14th inst., by Thos W. Harbin, Mr. Absolem Hide, to Mrs. Mary Putnam, all of Pickens District.

Issue of February 16, 1843
    Married on Thursday evening, the 8th inst., by William D. Steele, Esq., Mr. Henry A. Billingsley of Rabun Co., Ga., to Minerva Alexander, of Pickens District.

Issue of March 1, 1844
    Married on the evening of the 22d ult., by Wm. D. Steele, Esq., Mr. James Elliott to Miss Jane Rowland, all of Pickens District.
    Married on the same evening, by Rev. Wm. G. Mullinix, Mr. William Dowis to Miss Lucinda B. Thomas, all of Pickens District.
    Married on Thursday evening, the 15th inst., by Wm. D. Steele, Esq., Mr. James King to Miss Martha Jane, daughter of Samuel McClure, Esq., of Pickens District.
    Married on the evening, of the 18th inst., by the same, Mr. Elisha Gaines, to Miss Susannah, daughter of Gen. Garvin, all of Pickens Dist.
    Died on the 22d October 1843, George Ann, infant daughter of Mr. J. C. and Amanda Malvina Hall.
    Departed this life on Saturday last, Mrs. Amanda Malvina Hall, daugh-

74

ter of James Mullikin, Esq., and wife of J. C. Hall, in the 24th year of
her age.
   The Funeral of Benjamin Clement, deceased, will be preached by Wm.
P. Martin, on the 4th Lords Day in May next, at the House of Jane Clement,
4 miles south of Calhoun.

Issue of March 8, 1844
   Departed this life on Tuesday morning, the 27th ult., Mary Martha,
youngest daughter of Archibald and Emily C. Campbell, aged 6 years and
8 months.

Issue of March 15, 1844
   Died on the 11th inst., Kezia Miles, daughter of Mr. Rob't and Mary
Anderson of Pickens, aged 5 years and 8 months.

Issue of March 29, 1844
   Died, in the neighborhood of Centreville, on Saturday morning, March
2, in the 66th year of her age, Mrs. Elizabeth Reeves, consort of Mr.
John Reeves, of this District. (eulogy).
   Died in this city, on Saturday the 16th inst., at the residence of
Rev. Mr. Leavitt, Martha Jane, aged 6½ years, 2nd daughter of Rev. A.
Foster, East Constable, Franklin Co., N. Y. Providence (R. I.) Journal.

Issue of April 5, 1844
   Married on the 4th of April at St. Paul's Church, Pendleton, S. C.,
by the Rev. Wm. T. Potter, Dr. G. Jones Houston, of Lauderdale Co., Ala.,
to Miss Elizabeth A. M. Weyman, daughter of the late Joseph T. Weyman
of Charleston, and granddaughter of Samuel Marverick, Esq., of the former
place.
   Married in the 2nd Presbyterian Church yesterday, by Rev. Dr. Smyth,
Henry King McClintock, of Walterboro', to Mrs. Juliana Tovey, daughter
of the late Thos. A. Vardell, of this city. Char. Mercury, 29th of March.
   Married on Thursday evening, the 14th inst., by Gilbert D. Cere, Esq.,
Col. William R. Eaton, to Miss Nancy Louisa Harper, all of Covington
Co., Miss. Southern Journal.

Issue of April 26, 1844
   Died on Sunday morning, the 14th inst., Mr. Joseph Majors, aged
about 30. He has left a widow and one child.

Issue of May 10, 1844
   Married at the residence of Mr. S. P. Pickens, in this vicinty, on
Wednesday, the 24th inst., at 9 o'clock A. M., by the Rev. J. B. King,
the Rev. Leroi J. Halsey of Jackson, Miss., to Miss Caroline A. Anderson,
daughter of the late Col. Robert Anderson of Pendleton, S. C. Selma(Ala.)
Free Press, April 27.
   Married on Wednesday evening, the 1st inst.,by Rev. Wm. G. Mullenix,
Dr. Henry C. Miller of Abbeville to Miss Caroline V. Taliaferro, of
Anderson District.

Issue of May 17, 1844
   Another Revolutioner Gone. Departed this life, at the residence of
Capt. John Townes, in Polk Co., Tenn., on Sunday, the 28th April 1844, at
the advanced age of 93 years, Thomas Townes, a native of Amelia Co., Va.
...had the pleasure of seeing Cornwallis surrence his sword at Yorktown;
he afterwards emigrated to Greenville District, where he resided until
1835, when he moved to this State in company with his son...member of the
Baptist Church...the last of six brothers who were all soldiers of the
Revolution.

Issue of June 7, 1844
   Married on Tuesday, the 28th May, Mr. Jacob Tarrer to Miss Ardenia
Bremmer of Fredericksburg, Va.

Issue of June 14, 1844
   Died in the city of Philadelphia (where he had gone for the benefit
of his health), on the 4th inst., Dr. James Stuart, a native of Beaufort,
S. C., and for many years, a summer resident of this village...leaves a
wife of 33 years, and an aged mother. (eulogy).

Issue of June 21, 1844
Died on the 15th instant, Elvira, infant daughter of J. W. and Harriet Bridwell, aged 11 months and 15 days.

Issue of June 28, 1844
Married on Thursday evening, the 20th inst., in the Episcopal Church by the Rev'd William T. Potter, Dr. Charles L. Caillard, to Miss Eliza-beth M. Dart, all of Anderson District.

Issue of July 5, 1844
Departed this life on the 20th of June, at her residence near Pickens-ville, Mrs. Elizabeth Henderson, consort of James Henderson, aged 50 years. (eulogy).

Issue of July 19, 1844
Married on Tuesday, the 9th inst., by the Rev. James Wilson, Mr. Da-vid Wimpy to Miss Emily Moore, eldest daughter of Mr. Robert Moor, all of Anderson District.

Issue of August 30, 1844
Died on the morning of the 22d inst., Mrs. Eliza Browne, wife of Mr. Sidi H. Browne. She has left a husband and two children.

Issue of October 18, 1844
Married in this place, on the 6th inst., by the Rev. Mr. Barnes, Mr. Samuel J. Adams, to Miss Catherine Grant, of Pickens District.
Married on the 10th inst., by the Rev. Wm. G. Mullinix, Mr. Wm. A. Cox, of this place, to Miss Mary A. Adams, of Pickens District.
Died at his residence in Chickasaw Co., Miss., on the 4th September last, in the 60th year of his age, Mr. Thomas Gates, formerly a respect-able citizen of this district.

Issue of October 25, 1844
Married on the 17th inst., in DeKalb Co., Ga., by the Rev. John S. Wilson, Mr. James Steele of this district, to Miss Sarah C. Davis.

Issue of November 1, 1844
Died at his residence in Pickens District, on the 9th ult., Mr. William Simpson, in the 79th year of his age. Mr. S. had been a resident of the neighborhood where he died for about 40 years.
Died on Tuesday morning last, in Pickens District, Col. John Hunter, aged about 40 years.

Issue of November 29, 1844
Married on the 12th inst., by Rev. A. McGuffin, Mr. Leonard Capehart, to Miss Sarah Caradine, all of Pickens District.

Issue of December 6, 1844
Married in Charleston on the 22d ult., by Rev. Dr. Post, Mr. E. Sharpe, Jr. of this village to Miss Frances W., daughter of the late Gen. Robert Y. Hayne.

Issue of December 13, 1844
Died on the 8th inst., at Andersonville, Mrs. Sarah Harrison, wife of James Harrison, in the 54th year of her age.

Issue of December 20, 1844
Married on the 8th inst., by Rev. Wm. G. Mullinnix, Mr. Lewis Gil-strap to Miss Sarah A. Smith, all of Pickens District.
Married on the 12th inst., by the same, Mr. A. B. Grant, to Miss Leticia Thomas, all of Pickens District.

Issue of December 27, 1844
Married on the 10th inst., by the Rev. S. Vandiver, Mr. Ira Coffee to Miss Jane Miller, all of Pickens District.
Married on the 19th inst., by the Rev. G. W. Mullinax, Mr. Thos P. Campbell to Miss Macrina S. Arnold.

Issue of January 24, 1845
    Married on the 15th inst., by Rev. Mr. Pierce, Mr. Stephen M. Wilson
to Miss Elisabeth, daughter of Mr. Wm. C. Smith, all of this district.
    Married on the 16th by Rev. Mr. Humphreys, Mr. Elliott M. Keith of
Pickens, to Miss Mary Rebecca, youngest daughter of Mrs. E. Norris of
Anderson District.
    Married on the 16th by the Rev. Mr. Kennedy, Mr. William Martin, of
Abbeville, to Miss Mary, daughter of Col. David K. Hamilton, of this
district.
    Married on the 9th by the Rev. DR. N. Hoyt of Athens, the Hon. Fran-
cis W. Pickens of Edgefield, to Miss Marion A., second daughter of William
Dearing, Esq., of Charleston.

Issue of January 31, 1845
    Married on Tuesday, the 21st, by Rev. W. G. Mullinnex, Thomas H.
Gaines, only son of James Gaines dec'd, to Eliza Ann Hallum, all of
Pickens.
    Died at Greenwood in this District, on the 23d inst., Mr. James Smith
...left a wife and a number of children.
    Died on the 19th, Mr. Robert Gordon, in the 65th year of his age. He
was a native of Ireland, but came early to this country.
    Died on the 15th at Anderson, Mr. James Lawrence Maulden, a resident
of that village, aged 29.
    Died on Sunday evening, the 19th inst., Miss Frances Adella, eldest
daughter of David and Lydia McCroskey, aged about 22 years (eulogy).

Issue of February 7, 1845
    Died at his father's residence in this district, on Monday night,
Jan 27, 1845, Mr. Cyrus Gunnin, aged about 22 years, only son of James
Gunnin, Esq.
    Married on Tuesday the 28th ult., by Rev. J. L. Kennedy, Mr. Elijah E.
Alexander to Miss Vinetta Norton, all of Pickens district.
    Married on Dec. 31, 1844, John Sitton, Esq., of Oaktibbeha(sic) Co.,
Miss to Mrs. Eliza S. May of Noxubee Co., Miss.

Issue of February 14, 1845
    Mrs. Agnes Pickens, wife of Andrew C. Pickens, died near Pendleton at
29 years of age.

Issue of February 28, 1845
    Died on the 20th inst., near this place after a short but severe
illness, Mrs. Jane K. Ferrell in the 48th year of her age, wife of J. B.
Ferrell and daughter of Lewis and Susan Ogier dec. of Charleston, S. C.

Issue of March 7, 1845
    Died on Friday last at Pickensville, Stephen C. Reid, Esq., very
suddenly.
    Died on the same day, in Pickens District, Mr. J. F. Howell.
    Died on Sunday last, Mr. Giles Chapman, of Pickens District.
    Died on the 9th ult., at Greenville Village, the Hon. Waddy Thompson,
at the age of 75, formerly one of the Judges of the Court of Equity in
this State.
    Died on the 28th in Pickens District, Mr. William Alexander.

Issue of March 21, 1845
    Died at the residence of Mr. R. A. Maxwell, on the night of the 19th
instant, Mr. M. P. Earle, in the 41st year of his age. (eulogy).

Issue of April 4, 1845
    Married in Pickens District, on the 27th ult., by Tho. J. Humphreys,
Esq., Mr. Thomas L. Ballew to Miss Mary L., daughter of Maj. Henry Al-
bright of Floyd Co., Ga.
    Died at his residence in Pickens District, on Tuesday 25th March last,
Mr. David W. Hamilton, in the 65th year of his age, leaving a wife and
15 children. During the War of 1812, Mr. Hamilton served faithfully two
compaigns.

Issue of April 11, 1845
    Died at the residence of Mr. John S. Walker, in this vicinity, on the
26th March, George J. Bailey, aged 8 years, son of the late Isaac S. Bailey
of Charleston, S. C.

Issue of May 2, 1845
Died on the 21st ult of Pickens District, Mrs. _____ Dunlap, supposed
to be 102 years of age. She was born in Ireland, came young to this
country, and retained her health and her faculties in a remarkable degree
till near the close of life.
Died on the 24th ult., Mr. Fair Kirksey, merchant of this village, in
34th year of his age. (eulogy).
Departed this life on Saturday the 26th of April, John Harris, Esq.,
in the 84th year of his age. A tried soldier of the Revolution...leaves
a large family of children and grandchildren.

Issue of May 16, 1845
Married on Tuesday evening, the 11th inst., by Rev. B. Burroughs,
Captain Joseph Y. Fretwell, to Miss Nancy L., daughter of David Russell,
Esq., all of Anderson District.

Issue of May 23, 1845
Died on the 14th ult., Miss Eliza Caroline, eldest daughter of Josias
D. and Anne Gaillard, aged 20 years, 6 months and 14 days. In 1841, the
death of a sister...(long eulogy).
Died in Asheville, N. C., on Thursday, the 15th of May, Mrs. Elizabeth
Johnston, in the 69th year of her age. She was a native of Ireland, emi-
grated to this country in 1818, and settled in this District of which she
has been a resident ever since.

Issue of May 30, 1845
Married on the 21st of April, at Dudley, Mass., by the Rev. Dr. Bates,
the Rev'd James D. Butler of Burlington, Vt. to Miss Anna, daughter of
Dr. Bates.
Married on the 22d inst., by the Rev. W. G. Mullinix, Mr. William T.
Pickens, to Miss Julia A. F. Wilbern, of Anderson District.

Issue of June 27, 1845
Departed this life on the evening of the 21st, Mrs. Elizabeth M.
Gaillard, wife of Dr. Charles Gaillard...at the age of 22 years, but one
year a fondly beloved wife, and a few months a mother...member of the
Episcopal Church.

Issue of July 4, 1845
Died at this father's residence, on Monday the 23d ult., William P.
Bowden, son of James G. and Jane E. Bowden, aged three years and 13 days.

Issue of July 11, 1845
Died in Blairsville, Ga., on the 21st ult., in the 18th year of her
age, Elizabeth Fore, formerly Elizabeth Cook, of this place.

Issue of July 25, 1845
Married on the 16th inst., by H. E. Campbell, Esq., Mr. B. T. Rogers
to Miss S. Eaton.

Issue of September 12, 1845
Departed this life, on Tuesday the 12th ult., in Tippah Co., Miss.,
Mrs. Matilda McElroy, wife of Capt. John McElroy and daughter of Mr.
David Berry, decd., aged 35 years, 8 months, and 23 days. She left 7
children, husband, and mother...member of the Baptist Church for 18 years.

Issue of September 26, 1845
Died on the 12th August 1845, in the 30th year of his age, in Anderson District, Mr. James T. Harris, son of Joshua B. and Hannah Harris,
at his father's residence. (eulogy).

Issue of October 17, 1845
Died at his residence in this District on the 7th inst., Maj. Aaron
Broyles, in the 78th year of his age. He emigrated to this country, from
the State of Virginia, in early life and has resided at and near his
well known residence 60 years.
Died on the morning of the 12th inst., at his residence near this
place, Jesse P. Lewis, Esq., in the 51st year of his age...a native of
North Carolina, but for 30 years or more had made Pendleton his home...
member of the Presbyterian Church...wife and 6 children left behind.

78

Issue of October 24, 1845
Died on Monday last at his residence near this place, Mr. Benjamin
Smith, in the 70th year of his age. Mr. S. was a native of Charleston,
but removed to this distr'ct about 35 years ago.

Issue of November 7, 1845
Married on Thursday evening, the 16th ult., by the Rev. Jos. Crisham,
Mr. William Knox of Franklin Co., Ga., to Miss Eliza S. Berry, daughter
of William Berry, Esq., of Pickens District, S. C.
Married on Tuesday last in Pickens District, by Rev. Joseph Hillhouse,
the Rev. Dav[i]d Humphreys, of Anderson District, to Miss Mary, daughter
of the late Dr. Wm. Hunter, formerly of this place.

Issue of November 14, 1845
Married on the 30th October by the Rev. W. G. Mullinnix, Mr. John
G. Mullinnix, of Anderson, to Miss Elizabeth A. Gains, of Pickens.

Issue of November 28, 1845
Married on the 20th ult., by Rev. Wm. G. Mullinnex, Mr. John V. Majors
to Miss Sarah A. E. Holland.

Issue of December 12, 1845
Married on the 4th inst., by Rev. A. H. Cornish, Mr. W. H. D. Gaillard
to Miss Sally Taylor, eldest daughter of B. F. Sloan, Esq., all of this
District.
Married on the 7th inst., by Rev. Wm. G. Mullinnex, Mr. Wm. M., youngest son of Hundley and Elizabeth Evatt, to Miss Harriett N., youngest
daughter of Robert and Frances Gaines, all of Pickens.

Issue of January 9, 1846
Married on the 31st December by Rev. Wm. G. Mullinnex, Mr. Zachariah
Roland to Miss Elizabeth Newton of Anderson.
Died on the 24th ult., Mr. William Clayton senr., aged about 84 years,
a very old,very honest, and very industrious citizen of Pickens District.

Issue of January 16, 1846
Married on Tuesday evening, the 6th inst., by the Rev. John Bachman,
Mr. John C. DeGafferelly to Miss Jane S., eldest daughter of Capt. Thos.
F. Purse, all of Charleston. Charleston Courier.
Departed this life on Friday, the 2d inst., Mrs. Sarah Smith, consort
of Wm. C. Smith, residing near the village of Pendleton...member of the
Baptist Church.

Issue of January 23, 1846
Married on the 13th inst., by Rev. J. L. Kennedy, Mr. James Hunter
of Pendleton, to Miss Eliza J. Norton of Pickens.

Issue of February 6, 1846
Died on the 2nd inst., Mr. Anderson Burns, in the 51st year of his
age. (poem).

Issue of February 13, 1846
Married on the 3d February 1846, near Hickory Land, Pickens District,
S. C. by Livi N. Robins, Notary Public, Mr. C. M. Calhoon, to Miss Eliza-
beth McWhorter, all of Pickens.

Issue of February 27, 1846
Married on the 19th inst., by Rev. T. B. Madden, Mr. Levi Caldwell,
to Miss Sophia Goodin, all of Pickens District.

Issue of March 6, 1846
Married on the 19th February by Rev. W. G. Mullinnex, Mr. Greenberry
Crenshaw of Anderson, to Miss Sheba Ann Bolding, of Pickens.

Issue of March 13, 1846
Married on Sunday, the 8th inst., by David S. Taylor, Esq., Mr. John
Sims of Pickens District, to Miss Martha Manly Crenshaw, of Anderson
District.
Died at Choctaw Agency, Oaktibbeha(sic) Co., Miss., on the 27th Feb.
1846, Eliza S. Sitton, consort of John Sitton, Esq., formerly of Pendle-

ton, S. C. in the 34th year of her age...leaves husband and children...
member of the Baptist Church.

Issue of April 3, 1846
        Married on Thursday the 26th ult., by the Rev. R. Gaines, Mr. Aaron
G. Boggs, to Miss Marinda C. Mullinix, all of Pickens.
        Died on Tuesday, the 31st March, Mr. Elijah Mason, aged 40 (eulogy).

Issue of April 17, 1846
        Married on Sunday evening, the 12th inst., by Rev. Allen Faller, Mr.
Thomas A. Boggs, to Miss Sarah A. Campbell, daughter of Mr. Hanley
Campbell, all of Pickens District.
        Died at her residence in Greenville District, on the 8th March last,
Mrs. Elizabeth Bridwell, aged about 100 years.

Issue of May 1, 1846
        Died on the 20th April, Baylis Henry, second son of Doctor Joseph and
Anna F. Taylor, aged 4 years and 6 months.

Issue of May 15, 1846
        Married on Tuesday, the 12th inst., by the Rev. Mr. Phillip Elrod,
Mr. Wm Slatter, to Miss Caroline Barkley, all of Anderson District.

Issue of May 29, 1846
        Died at the residence of his son, Charles Gates Jun'r, Greene Co.,
Ala., on Sunday the 10th inst., Mr. Charles Gates Sen'r, in the 86th
year of his age. He was a native of Virginia, and served two campaigns
in the war of the Revolution. He removed to S. C., and was one of the
first residents of Pendleton District, where he lived for many years.

Issue of June 5, 1846
        Died at his residence, in Lafayette Co., Miss., on the 28th January,
1846, Mr. James M. Duff, in the 38th year of his age...member of the
Presbyterian Church(eulogy).
        Died on Friday morning, at 8 o'clock, the 15th in the vicinity of
Centreville, Mr. John Reeves, aged 67 years. He resided in this district
nearly 60 years, but was a native of Granville Co., N. C....member of the
Methodist Episcopal Church at Sandysprings...(eulogy).

Issue of July 3, 1846
        Married on the 28th inst., by H. E. Campbell, Esq., Mr. Richard
Collins, (aged about 16), to Miss Susannah Russell (aged about 52), all
of Pickens District.
        Died on the 19th of June, Mrs. Jane F. Owen, wife of Frederick Owen,
in the 84th year of her age, leaving her husband and seven children...
(eulogy).
        Died in Pontotoc Co., Miss., on the 30th ult., Mrs. Martha Sloan, wife
of William D. Sloan (eulogy).

Issue of July 24, 1846
        Died on Sabbath the 21st of June, Mr. Matthew Martin, in the 34th
year of his age...member of the Presbyterian Church...He left behind a
Father and Mother with seven brothers, four of whom were then lying upon
beds of affliction, and two sisters, one of which Mary E. has since died.
(eulogy).

Issue of July 31, 1846
        Died of devility, July 15, 1846, at this residece in Pickens District,
James H. Dendy, Esq., an elder in the Presbyterian Richland Church for
some years, and acted as Ordinary of Pickens District for 16 years...He
left a large family...(eulogy).

Issue of August 7, 1846
        Died on the 2d of June last, in Memphis, Tenn., Mrs. Cynthia T.
Miller, consort of Mr. George Miller, in the 44th year of her age.

Issue of August 14, 1846
        Married on Thursday evening, the 6th August, at ½ past three, by Rev.
W. G. Mullinix, Mr. E. B. Gassaway to Miss Artemesa Lawrence.
        Married on the same evening, at half past seven, by the same, Mr. J.
N. Boggs, to Miss Catharine I. Gaines, last single daughter of J. Gaines,

80

decd.

Issue of August 28, 1846
Died recently in Edgefield District, Thos J. Hibble, Esq., formerly
a member of the Legislature from this district, and at his death, a can-
didate for the State Senate.
Died in Abbeville, Archibald H. Arnold, Esq.

Issue of September 4, 1846
Died at Carlyle, Cumberland Co., Penn., on Tuesday morning, the 18th
August, Mr. Thos Hunter, aged 28 years.

Issue of September 11, 1846
Died on the 21st July last, Mrs Sarah Grant, in the 65th year of her
age...(eulogy).

Issue of November 13, 1846
Died on Wednesday last, the 14th October, Reuben Grisham, in the 38th
year of his age. He was a antive of Pendleton, S. C., bur during the last
18 years a resident of this place. He has left a wife and a large family
of young children...Thibodaux (La.) Minerva.

Issue of November 20, 1846
Died on Saturday morning last, Dr. E. W. Kirksey, aged 72. In the
spring of 1843, he turned his attention to the study of medicine...he
graduated from the University of New York in the spring of 1845....

Issue of November 27, 1846
Married on the 17th inst., by Wm. S. Grisham, Esq., Mr. Joshua Barton,
of Cass Co., Ga., to Miss Catharine Moore, of Pickens District, S. C.

Issue of December 4, 1846
Married on Nov. 26, by Rev. Wm. G. Mullinnex, Mr. Reuben Arnold, to
Miss Matilda McDow, all of Pickens.
Married in this village, on Tuesday evening last, by the Rev. Wm. H.
Moore, Samuel P. Adams of the "Chambers Herald" and Miss Mary A., only
daughter of Wm. L. Crayton, Esq., all of this place. Chambers (Ala.)
Herald.

Issue of December 25, 1846
Married on the evening of the 17th inst., by E. M. Keith, Esq., Mr.
William Brewster to Miss Elizabeth, daughter of Dan'l M. Alexander, all
of Pickens District.
Married on the same evening by Wm. D. Steele, Esq., Mr. George Elli-
ott to Miss Nancy Hunnicutt, all of Pickens District.
Married on the same evening by Rev. Wm. G. Mullinex, George W. McDow,
Esq., to Miss Mary Margaret Lawrence, all of Pickens District.
Died on Sunday morning, the 29th ult., of Scarlet Fever, Martha Susan,
only children of John A. and Susan C. Simpson, formerly of Anderson
District, S. C., but now of Tippah Co., Miss., aged 2 years, 2 months,
and 14 days.

Issue of January 1, 1847
Married in this village, on Sunday last, in the M. E. Church, by the
Rev. Wm. G. Mullinex, Mr. George Washington Crogan to Miss Sarah Ann
Burns.
Married on the 24th ult., by W. S. Grisham, Esq., Mr. Daniel Brewer
to Miss Rinela Caldwell, all of Pickens District, S. C.

Issue of January 22, 1847
Died on Friday evening, the 15th inst., in the 43d year of her age,
Mrs. Sarah S. Symmes, wife of Dr. F. W. Symmes, of this place...left a
husband and six children...(eulogy).
Died at LaFayette, Chambers Co., Ala., on the 25 December last, in
the 54th year of her age., Mrs. Cynthia Adams, widow of Mr. John Adams,
formerly of this place...member of the Presbyterian Church.

Issue of January 29, 1847
Married at Pickens C. H., on Tuesday evening, 19th January 1847, by
Rev. J. L. Kennedy, Mr. James George to Miss Mary Telford, all of Pickens.

Issue of February 19, 1847
Died on the 10th February in the 57th year of her age, Mrs. Susannah Cherry, relict of the late Samuel Cherry of Pendleton...for many years a member of the Presbyterian Church.
Died on the 9th January, Mrs. McElroy, consort of Mr. Archibald McElroy, in this vicinity.
Bailey Barton, Esq., a well known resident of Pickens District, died in the early part of last week (we have not learned certainly what day), aged about 52. For several years, he represented this District in the State Legislature.

Issue of March 5, 1857
Married on the 25th February, by the Rev. Mr. Dickson, Mr. James Y. Sitton, of this place, to Miss Harriet D. David of Abbeville.
Married on Tuesday evening last at Anderson C. H., by Rev. W. D. Mullinix, Dr. Charles Lewis Gaillard, to Mrs. Althea Louisa Creswell.

Issue of March 12, 1847
Married on the 8th inst., by W. S. Grisham, Esq., Mr. Jacob Fricks, to Miss Rebecca Calhoun, all of Pickens District.

Issue of March 19, 1847
Died at Decatur, Ga., on the 26th February, Dr., Thomas W. Alexander of Laurensville, in the 58th year of his age. Dr. A. was native of Greenville District in this state.

Issue of March 26, 1847
Died on Thursday morning, the 18th March 1847, at the residence of her father near Pendleton, Susan Bullein, daughter of Barnard E. Bee.

Issue of April 23, 1847
Died at her late residence in Chambers Co., Ala., near West Point, on Sunday the 4th inst., Mrs. Susannah Story, widow of the late Charles Story, in the 73d year of her age...for more than 50 years, a member of the Presbyterian Church.

Issue of April 30, 1847
Died on Sunday morning, the 18th inst., at Townville, Anderson District, S. C., Rev. Sanford Vandiver, in the 60th year of his age.

Issue of May 28, 1847
Married on the 13th inst., by W. S. Grisham, Esq., Capt. Levi M. Crenshaw to Miss Martha, daughter of Wm. Abbett, all of Pickens District.
Died in Philadelphia, Miss., on the 1st May 1847, Lewis Mauldin, in the 53d year of his age. The deceased was a native of Union District, S. C....for 22 years a member of the M. E. Church...leaves a wife and four children....

Issue of June 11, 1847
Died on Saturday, the 5th inst., at her residence in Anderson District, Mrs. Jane Harris, wife of Andrew Harris, aged 59 years, 4 months, and 21 days.

Issue of June 18, 1847
Married at Pendleton, on Tuesday evening last, by David S. Taylor, Esq., Mr. Thomas Christian to Miss ____ Frazier.

Issue of June 25, 1847
Died on the 4th inst., at the residence of Mrs. Martha Lawrence, in Pickens District, Mrs. Laura C., wife of Thomas R. Brackenridge, aged 32. One child only, survives her, too young to feel the extent of his loss.

Issue of July 16, 1847
Married on the 13th inst., by Rev. B. F. Mauldin, Joseph E. Brown, Esq., of Canton, Geo. to Miss Elizabeth, daughter of Rev. Joseph Grisham of West Union, S. C.

Issue of July 23, 1847
Died on the 14th ultimo, in Talladega Co., Ala., Mrs. Eliza Howard, consort of Capt. Jon Howard, in the 33d year of her age. She, with her

82

husband, was born and raised in Anderson District, S. C. and moved to
Alabama in the fall of 1845 (eulogy).

Issue of July 30, 1847
    Married on the 26 July, by Miles M. Norton, Esq., Mr. Matthew Carson
to Mrs. Jane Hays, all of Pickens.

Issue of August 6, 1847
    Married on the 29 July, by Rev'd W. G. Mullinex, of Pickens, Mr.
Larkins Newton to Miss Ruth M. Welborn, both of Anderson District.

Issue of August 20, 1847
    Married on the 12th inst., by W. S. Grisham, Esqr., Mr. Silas B.
Fricks to Miss Milly Matilda Calhoun, all of Pickens.

Issue of August 27, 1847
    Married on the 22d inst., by the Rev. Tyre B. Mauldin, Mr. Andrew E.
Finley to Miss Arminda, daughter of Martin Moss, all of Pickens.
    Married on Thursday evening, the 12th inst.,by W. D. Steele, Esq.,
Mr. Joab Lewis, from Cass Co., Ga., to Miss Phalba L.,daughter of the
late Bailey Barton, Esq., of Pickens District.
    Died at the residence of Gov. Drew, in this city, on Tuesday, 27th
of July, Col. Andrew Hammond, in the 25th year of his age. The dec'd was
born in Pendleton District, S. C. He removed to this state, and lived
for some time in Jackson, Laurence Co., where he had the office of Post-
master & subsequently Clerk of Court. In 1844, he was appointed Aid-de-
Camp to the Governor, with the rank of Colonel of Cavalry...(eulogy)
Little Rock (Ark.) Banner.

Issue of September 17, 1847
    Married on the 26th Augustlast, by the Rev. W. G. Mullinex, Mr. John
C. Rush to Miss Mary A. J. DuFreese.
    Married on the 12th inst., by the Rev. Wm. M. Morton, Mr. W. H. How-
ard to Miss Margaret C. Barnes, all of Pickens District.
    Died at his residence in Madison Co., Fla., on the 18th inst., James
M. Sloan, a native of this District...member of the Baptist Church.
    Died on Saturday night, September 4, between the hours of 11 and 12,
Louisa Caroline Morris, consort of Richard M. Morris, in the vicinity of
Sandy-springs Camp ground, aged 30 years, 1 month and 13 days.

Issue of October 15, 1847
    Married on the 7th inst., by Rev. John Zimmerman, Mr. Andrew Middle-
ton Norris, to Miss Mary E., daughter of Capt. William Steele, all of
Anderson District.

Issue of October 22, 1847
    Married near Columbia, Miss., on the 18th September by James Lott,
Esq., the Rev. H. T. Lewis (late of Pendleton, S. C.) to Miss Ann C.
Murray, of Gainesville, Miss. Marion, (Ala.)News.
    Married on the 3d inst., by Rev'd W. G. Mullinix, George G. Hopson of
Georgia to Miss Malinda M. Davis of Anderson.
    Married by the same, on the 17th inst., Dr. A. Elrod to Miss Leander
E. Morris.

Issue of October 29, 1847
    Married on the 21st ult., by T. B. Mauldin, Esq., Mr. Henry M. Garner
to Miss Caroline Blalock.
    Married on the 12th inst., by the same, Samuel Horseley, Esq., to
Miss Rachel Ramply, all of Pickens District, S. C.

Issue of November 5, 1847
    Married on the 21st of last month, by the Rev. A. W. Poss, Mr. Newton
Harper, to Miss Martha Millwee.

Issue of November 19, 1847
    Departed this life on Wednesday the 10th inst., at his late residence
in this District, Major James Watson, in the 83d year of his age. He
has long been a resident of this District, having lived on the place
where he died 50 years...member of the Presbyterian Church.

Issue of November 26, 1847
Married on the 15th inst., by Rev. W. G. Mullinix of Pickens, Agusta
W. Walker of Geo., to Miss Maria T. Richardson of Anderson District.
Married by the same, on Thursday evening, Mr. Joberry Caradine, to
Miss Susan E. Frederick, all of Pickens.
Died in Franklin Co., Ga., on the 12th inst., at 12 o'clock PM, at
the residence of her father, David Smith, Mrs. Sarah E. Bryan, wife of
F. C. Bryan, aged 16 years, 8 months, and 4 days (eulogy).

Issue of December 3, 1847
Married on Thursday evening, Nov. 25, by the Rev. G. W. Boggs, Mr.
Wallace H. Miller to Miss Laura E. Miller.

Issue of December 10, 1847
Married on the 8th inst., by the Rev. W. G. Mullinix, of Pickens, Mr.
Wm. B. Cherry to Miss Sarah M. Lewis, both of Anderson.
Married on the 5th instant, at 5 o'clock PM, by W. S. Grisham, Esq.,
Mr. Anderson Ivester to Miss Arzela, daughter of Martin Moss, all of
Pickens.

Issue of December 31, 1847
Married on the 21st December 1847, by the Rev. Henry Tyler, of Elbert
Co., Ga., Mr. C. H. Speares of Franklin Co., Ga., to Miss Susanna Adaline
Terrell, daughter of Mr. Aaron Terrell of Pickens District, S. C.

Issue of January 14, 1848
Died at Salubrity, in Pickens District, on Friday, 31st December last,
Mrs. Harriet B. Williams, wife of Wm. S. Williams, and daughter of Thomas
Worthington, late of Newberry District, decd, in the 31st year of her age
...leaves a husband and three children...(eulogy).

Issue of January 21, 1848
Died in Pickens District, on the 10th inst., Mrs. Casendine Shelor,
wife of Joseph R. Shelor, in her 30th year...member of the Presbyterian
Church...left a mother, husband, and five children.

Issue of January 28, 1848
Married at Orrville, on Thursday evening, the 30th ult., by Rev. J.
L. Kennedy, Mr. Gustavus J. Orr of Jefferson, Ga., to Miss Caroline, eld-
est daughter of Dr. Wm. and Mary D. Anderson.

Issue of February 4, 1848
Married on Thursday, the 27th January 1848, by Rev. W. G. Mullinix,
Mr. Nathaniel M. Madden, to Miss Mary A. Garvin.

Issue of February 11, 1848
Married in Pickens District, on the 27th inst., by John Knox, Esq.,
Mr. E. M. Perry to Miss Mary Cannon, all of Pickens District.
Married near Hickory Land, on Thursday the 3d inst., by L. W. Robins,
Esq., Mr. John Wilson to Miss Caroline McWhorter, all of Pickens District.
Married on the 2d inst., by W. S. Grisham, Esq., Mr. John H. Dorsey,
to Miss Sarah, daughter of Daniel E. Riley, all of Pickens District.
Married on the 1st inst., by Rev. W. G. Mullinix, Mr. Epps Williams,
to Miss Mary Thomas, all of Pickens.

Issue of February 18, 1848
Married on Monday evening, the 14th inst., by John B. Sitton, Esq.,
Mr. David H. Hopkins, of Pickens District, to Miss M. Mills.
Died in the village of Anderson, on the 24th January last, Mrs. Rebecca E. S. Webb, consort of Elijah Webb, Esquire, in the 35th year of
her age...left a husband and two step-children and one infant of her
own...(long eulogy).

Issue of March 3, 1848
Married on the 24th February by Rev. W. G. Mullinix, Mr. Gideon
Ellis Jun'r to Miss Susannah A. McWhorter, all of Pickens.

Issue of March 17, 1848
Departed this life (near Townville) in Pickens District, S. C. on
the 24th inst., Jesse, youngest son of Charles and Milly Hunt, aged 27
years and 10 days...left aged parents and several brothers and sisters.

Issue of March 24, 1848
    Married on the 2d inst., by E. M. Keith, Esq., Mr. Francis M. Hunni-
cutt to Miss Frances Caroline, daughter of Wm. Hunnicutt, all of Pickens
District.
    Married on the 16th March by Rev. WM. G. Mullinix, Mr. Wm. J. Smith
to MIss Martha Hamilton.
    Married in the village of Pendleton, on the morning of the 23d inst.,
by Rev. Mr. Cornish, Dr. Thomas L. Lewis to Eliza C., daughter of John
Maxwell.

Issue of April 28, 1848
    Married on the evening of the 11th instant, by Rev. A. W. Ross, Maj.
J. D. Wright of Laurens to Miss Anna, daughter of Mr. R. A. Maxwell.

Issue of May 12, 1848
    Married on Wednesday evening, May 10, by the Rev. Mr. Cornish, Mr.
Clement H. Stevens of Charleston to Miss Anne F., daughter of Hon.
Barnard E. Bee, near Pendleton.

Issue of May 19, 1848
    Died at Pendleton on the 8th inst., Robert Hayne, infant son of Elan
and Frances H. Sharpe, aged 5 months and 21 days.

Issue of May 26, 1848
    Married on Tuesday, the 16th inst., by the Rev. J. Hillhouse, Mr. A.
Hester, to Miss Emily Deane, both of Pickens District.
    Married by the same, on Thursday, Mr. Wm. P. Norris to Miss S. R.
Steele, all of Anderson District.

Issue of June 2, 1848
    Married on the 21st May, by John Knox, Esq., Mr. Manuel Hedden to
Miss Elisabeth Fox, both of Macon Co., N. C.

Issue of June 16, 1848
    Married on the 1st inst., by Rev. J. Hillhouse, Mr. A. L. McElroy,
to Miss Sarah R. Belott, all of Anderson District.
    Married on the 8th inst., by Rev. J. L. Kennedy, Mr. Samuel Easley,
to Miss Elizabeth F. Sloan, of this Village.
    Died on the 30th May, Mrs. Elizabeth McPherson, in the 70th year of
her age.
    Died on the 6th of June, Othneil, in the 16th year of his age, son of
Samuel and Malinda McGee.
    Died on the 7th June, Mrs. Dorcas McPherson, in the 57th year of her
age.

Issue of June 23, 1848
    Married at Horse Shoe, on the 11th inst., by Rev. Joseph Grisham,
David Dickson, Esq., to Miss Frances, eldest daughter of Edward Hughes,
Esq., all of Pickens District, S. C.
    Died at her residence near Bachelor's Petreat, on Sunday evening, the
7th ult., Mrs. Sarah Fullerton, consort of John Fullerton, late of Pickens district, in the 88th year of her age...She was a native of Antrim
County, Ireland, but for the last 30 years, a resident of Pickens District. For upwards of 60 years, a member of the Presbyterian Church.

Issue of July 7, 1848
    Departed this life, Agatha Maverick, at San Antonio, Texas, on 9 May
...aged seven years and nearly one month, the eldest daughter of S. A.
and Mary A. Maverick.

Issue of July 21, 1848
    Died at her father's residence in this District on Thursday, 13th
July, Miss Drucilla Philips, after a long and painful illness, in the
36th year of her age.

Issue of August 4, 1848
    Married on the 28th June by Rev. Mr. Bailey, C. E. Broyles of Pendle-
ton to Miss L. A. Johnson of Barnwell.
    Died on Sunday evening, the 30th July at the residence of her father
near Pendleton, Emma Templer, youngest daughter of Barnard E. Bee.

Issue of August 11, 1848
    William Hineman was killed in Pickens District last week by Toliver Smith.

Issue of August 25, 1848
    Married on the 13th inst., by John Knox, Esq., At Chattoga old Town, Mr. Isaac Holden to Miss Jinny Nicholson, all of Pickens.

Issue of September 1, 1848
    Married near Hickory Land, Pickens District, S. C. on Tuesday, the 22d August 1848, by L. N. Robins, Esq., Mr. Jacob Fricks to Miss Elizabeth Head.
    Died at Mr. Joseph Watkins' residence, on Monday the 21st of August 1848, Mrs. Dinah Passmore, in the 82d year of her age.

Issue of September 15, 1848
    Married on Tuesday the 5th inst., by Rev. Jesse Dean, Mr. Augustin L. Garvin of Hall Co., Ga., to Miss Emma J. Clayton, of Pickens District, S. C.
    Married on the 10th inst., by Rev. W. G. Mullinex, Mr. John T. Freeman to Miss Jane E. Mullikin.

Issue of September 29, 1848
    Married on the 17th inst., by A. Alexander, Esq., Mr. Hiram J. Grogan of Cass Co., Ga., to Miss Sarah Adaline, daughter of James Roberson, of Pickens District.

Issue of October 6, 1848
    Married on the 26th ult., by W. G. Mullinex, of Pickens, Mr. Wm. A. Mullinex of Aberdeen, Miss., to Miss Sylvania A. Boggs of Pickens.
    Died at the residence of her husband in Choctaw County, Mrs. Frances Caroline, consort of H. Bardine, Esq., in the 29th year of her age. She was the daughter of John and Frances Sitton, formerly of Pendleton District, S. C. She early attached herself to the M. E. Church...She left a husband and seven children. Miss. Telegraph.
    Died at the residence of her husband in Oktibbeha Co.[Miss.], on Thursday, the 17th inst., Mrs. Jane, consort of Percival P. Holbert, Esq.

Issue of October 20, 1848
    Married on the 12th inst., by A. Alexander, Esq., Mr. Leonard Rogers to Miss Pamelia Sneed, all of Pickens District.
    Departed this life on 1 October 1848 at his residence in Cobb Co., Ga., Mr. Benjamin Smith, in the 61st year of his age...long a member of the Presbyterian Church.

Issue of October 27, 1848
    Married on Tuesday evening, the 17th inst., in the Village of Pickens, by Rev. J. L. Kennedy, Dr. Jos. N. Lawrence to Miss Lucretia Alexander.
    Died at Cassville, Ga., on the 10th inst., Mrs. Phebe Christian, formerly of Pendleton, S. C. in the 43d year of her age, leaving a husband and seven children.

Issue of November 3, 1848
    Died in this city, on the 5th inst., Mr. Henry G. Daniels, in the 48th year of his age. He was a native of Greenville, S. C., previous to his removal to this city (1840), had resided several years in Winchester, Va...member of the Baptist Church...leaves an amiable widow and numerous friends. Montgomery (Ala.) Journal.

Issue of November 17, 1848
    Married on Thursday the 9th November 1848, by Rev. Mr. Parker, Mr. Wesley Graham to Miss. _____ Jeans, all of Pickens, S. C.
    Married on the 26th ult.,by E. M. Keith, Esq., Mr. Thomas S. Roe to Miss Anna B. Newton, all of Pickens.
    Married on the 15th September 1846(sic) by John Nance, Esq., Mr. Edward Honea to Miss Caroline Davis, all of Pickens, S. C.
    Died at the residence of Mr. Thomas R. Cherry, in this Village, on the night of the 11th inst., Dr. Edwin Reese in the 75th year of his age. (eulogy).

Issue of November 24, 1848
    Married on the 15th November 1848, by Rev. John S. Henley, Rev. Benjamin B. Parker of Franklin Co., Ga., to Miss Jane Tyler of Fibert Co., Ga.
    Married on Thursday, the 16th inst., by Rev. A. W. McGuffin, Mr. Henry Goodwin to Miss E. Rouse, all of Pickens District.

Issue of December 1, 1848
    Married in Monroe, Ga., on Nov. 2, by Rev. H. P. Pitchford, Mr. G. S. Alexander of Cassville, Ga., and Miss Celestia A., daughter of R. Rogers of the former place. Athens (Ga.) Banner.

Issue of December 8, 1848
    Died at his residence in Pickens District, on the 22d November, Mr. Elias Hollingsworth, in the 87th year of his age.

Issue of December 15, 1848
    Died at her residence, Nov. 1, in Cobb Co., Ga., Mrs. Mary Smith, consort of Benjamin Smith, who was taken to rest just one months before her. The deceased had passed 54 years pilgrimate on Earth and had endeared herself to numerous acquaintances in Anderson District, S. C., where she was a resident until 1844.

Issue of December 22, 1848
    Married on the 14th ult, by Rev. W. G. Mullinex, Mr. John M. Evins, of Georgia, to Miss Jane E. Garvin of Pickens District.
    Married on Thursday, the 7th of this inst., by J. B. E. Caradine, Esq., Mr. Benjamin F. Burkett, to Miss Elizabeth K. McDaniel, all of Pickens District.
    Married on Wednesday evening, the 13th inst., by Rev. J. R. Hillhouse, Mr. J. S. Cunningham of Union District, to Miss Mary G. Hillhouse, of Anderson.
    Departed this life at Hickory Hill, in Siline Co., Arkansas, on 8 November, Mrs. Martha C. Martin, consort of James H. Martin, and daughter of John B. and Francis Hammond.

Issue of December 29, 1848
    Married on the 19th inst., by W. G. Mullinix, Mr. Stephen Martin, to Miss Rosemalinda McKinney.
    Married on the 21st inst., by the same, Mr. B. F. Evatt to Miss Jane Martin.
    Married on Thursday, the 21st inst., by J. B. E. Carradine, Esq., Mr. Baylis R. Rice to Miss Elizabeth Purket.

Issue of January 5, 1849
    Married on Thursday, the 14th ult., by Rev. N. P. Morgan, Mr. Micajah F. Berry of Elbert Co., Ga., to Miss Eletha A. Spencer, of Green Co., Ala.

Issue of January 12, 1849
    Married on Tuesday, the 26th December, by Rev. Jeremiah Ingold, Mr. Zion Bredwell of Chesterville, S. C. to Miss Catharine J. Cremminger of Cabarros (sic) Co., N. C.
    Married on the seventh instant, by Rev. Simeon Hembree, Mr. Burgess H. Cox, to Miss Laura Hardin, all of Pickens District.
    Died at his residence in Pickens District, on the 23d November 1848, Mr. Henry Garner, in the 74th year of his age. He was born in Randolph Co., N. C....joined Baptist Church...(eulogy).

Issue of January 19, 1849
    Died on Friday, the 5th inst., at his residence in Anderson District, Mr. Joseph Watkins, in the 66th year of his age...member of the Baptist Church...(eulogy).

Issue of January 26, 1849
    Married on the 17th inst., by Rev. W. G. Mullinnex, Wm. Russel to Miss Rebecca Colton.
    Married on the 18th inst., by the same, David White to Miss Mariah McMillan.
    Departed this life on the 5th inst., at this place, Mrs. Catharine

Adaline Presley, wife of A. M. presly, and daughter of Horatio and Margaret Reese...21 years old on New Year's Day...left an infant son, 26 days old. (eulogy) [torn].

Issue of February 2, 1849
Married on the 31st ult., by the Rev. W. G. Mullennix, Mr. Richard M. Morris, to Miss Sarah M. Wigington.
Died in Pickens District, S. C., Mrs. Mary K. Campbell, consort of Hundley E. Campbell and 4th daughter of Jas. Gaines, decd., in the 40th year of her age. For near 30 years, member of the Methodist Episcopal Church...(eulogy).

Issue of February 23, 1849
Died at his residence in this village, on the 15th inst., Richard T. Wilson...in the 45th year of his age, a residence of our Village for near 20 years...left a wife and 6 small children.

Issue of March 9, 1849
Peter R. Boss, died at Mr. L. S. Hamilton's, near this place, on the 26th ult., about 60 years of age. He stated before his death that his home was in Richland District, and he had a mother and brothers living in Pennsylvania. He was decently buried in the Episcopal burying ground, by the Masonic fraternity. Geo. Seaborn.

Issue of March 16, 1849
Departed this life at this residence in Lauderdale Co., Ala., Mr. Joseph Thompson, on the 25th day of Jan. last, after an illness of 10 days.

Issue of March 23, 1849
Married on the 14th inst., by the Rev. D. Simmons, Capt. B. F. Dickson to Miss M. Gantt, all of Anderson.

Issue of March 30, 1849
Another Revolutionary Patriot Gone. Died at his residence in Albemarle Co., Va., on Thursday last, March 8, Mr. Jesse Lewis, in the 86th year of his age. Mr. Lewis was born May 13, 1763, and at the age of 16 entered the Revolutionary army. On 13 Apr 1786, he was married to Miss Nancy Clarkson, who survives him. Their descendants to the 5th generation reside in the county. (eulogy). Charlottesville (Va.) Republican.

Issue of April 6, 1849
Died, suddenly, at his residence in Anderson District, on the 19th ult., Andrew J. Liddell, Esq., in the 64th year of his age, leaving a widow, 4 daughters and a number of grandchildren...for 35 or 36 years held the office of Magistrate...Ruling Elder in Mount Zion Church. (eulogy).

Issue of April 13, 1849
Died, on the 27th March, at the residence of W. G. Mullinnex, Mrs. Nancy Gaines. She left home on the 12th March to visit her son-in-law (W. G. Mullinex) and was taken on the 15th with a sore throat...50 years a member of the Methodist Episcopal Church.

Issue of April 20, 1849
Married at Whetstone, on the 12th inst., by Sam'l Moseley, Esq., James Evans to Louisa, daughter of Hubert Quarles, all of Pickens District.
Died on Monday, the 9th inst., at High Shoals, Anderson District, in the 40th year of his age, Mr. Benjamin Mason...member of the Baptist Church...left a wife and six small children (eulogy).

Issue of April 27, 1849
Married on the 15th inst., by John Knox, Esq., of Pickens District, Mr. A. Edwards to Miss Elizabeth Queen, both of Macon Co., N. C.
Married on the 17th inst., by the Rev. Wm. M. Moton, Mr. Jacob Chamberlin, aged 70 to Miss Judy Chastain, aged 16, all of Pickens District.
Married on the 15th inst., by Miles M. Norton, Esq., Mr. Joseph Mauldin, to Miss Sarah Ann Powers, all of Pickens District.

88

Issue of May 4, 1849
    Died at his residence in Pickens District, on the 28th ultimo, Mr.
Joseph Taylor, in the 49th year of his age.
    Departed this life, on the evening of the 23d ult., Mr. William G.
Hamilton, son of David W. and Mary Hamilton, at the early age of 21 years
and 11 months.

Issue of May 11, 1849
    Married on the 30th ult., by J. B. E. Caradine, Esq., Mr. Dempsy Yow
to Miss Mary Balding, both of Pickens District.
    Married on the 3d inst., by the Rev. Wm. G. Mullinex, Mr. James John-
son to Miss Sarah Newton, both of Anderson District.

Issue of May 18, 1849
    Married on the 7th inst., by A. Alexander, Esq., Mr. Geo. W. A. Smith
to Miss Martha Jane, daughter of John G. Maulden, all of Pickens District.
    Died at the residence of his sister, Mrs. Mays, on the 16th inst.,
Edward H. Earle, in the 28th year of his age. (eulogy).
    Died on the 13th inst., Mrs. Nancy T. Lewis, daughter of Mrs. Jesse
P. Lewis, in the 24th year of her age. (eulogy).

Issue of May 25, 1849
    Died on the 12th of May, in the27th year of his age, Mrs. Sarah Ann,
consort of Maj. Willis Robinson...left a husband and one child.

Issue of June 1, 1849
    Married on the 15th ult., by Wm. S. Grisham, Esq., Mr. Andrew J.
Dorsey, to Miss Nancy Isabella Colhoun, all of Pickens District.
    Married on the 15th ult., by Rev. J. B. Hillhouse, Mr. Henry R. Hughes
to Miss Elizabeth F. Dendy, daughter of James H. Dendy, decd, all of
Pickens District.

Issue of June 8, 1849
    Departed this life, Augusta Maverick, daughter of Sam'l Augustus
Maverick at San Antonio, Texas, on the 24th April 1849, aged 5 years,
10 months, and 24 days.

Issue of June 15, 1849
    Dr. Henry H. Townes, died at his residence in Abbeville District, on
Wednesday, the 30th ult., aged 44 years, 8 months, and 26 days...a native
of Greenville District, where his mother and brothers now reside...stu-
died medicine with the late Dr. Richard Harrison...first settled at
Countsville, Lexington District. Afterwards he resided 2 or 3 years in
Greenville and for nearly 20 years, has been a resident of Abbeville
District...(eulogy). Greenville Mountaineer.

Issue of July 6, 1849
    Married on Tuesday morning, the 3d of July, at Woodland, near Pendle-
ton, by Rev'd A. H. Cornish, Dr. John C. Calhoun Jr., son of the Hon.
J. C. Calhoun, to Miss Annzie R., eldest daughter of the late Rev'd
Jasper Adams, all of Pickens District.
    Died in Pickens District, June 30th, Mrs. Rebecca Verner, aged 75...
born in Pennsylvania, and after residing in Iredell, N. C., removed to
this state in 1792. She was married to John Verner, Esq., the next
year, having been his consort 56 years...(eulogy).

Issue of July 20, 1849
    James Awbler Sen., a citizen of Pickens District, departed this life,
26 June 1849, being over 90 years of age. He was a Virginian by birth,
and a graduate of William and Mary College. He came to Edgefield District, S. C. and engaged as a teacher in private families...He spent the
last 26 years of his life in Pickens District. (eulogy).Pickens Courier.

Issue of August 10, 1849
    Departed this life, on Monday evening, the 16th July, at his father's
residence in Anderson District, Major John James Norris, aged 25 years,
6 months, and 27 days. Anderson Gazette.

Issue of August 24, 1849
    Married on the 9th inst., by Rev. Wm. G. Mullinnex, Mr. H. E. Camp-

bell to Miss Frances Arnold, all of Pickens District.

Issue of August 31, 1849
    Married on the 9th of August by Rev. James Boswell, Mr. Wm. D. Sloan, to Miss Margaret Caroline, eldest daughter of Mr. George Houlditch, all of Pontotoc Co., Miss.

Issue of September 7, 1849
    Married on the 30th ult., by the Rev. W. G. Mullennix, Mr. Wm. G. Chapman, to Miss Sarah Smith.
    Died in Benton Co., Ala., on the 7th ult., Mr. Joseph Pinson, formerly, for many years a resident of this Village. (eulogy).

Issue of September 14, 1849
    Died at his residence in this village, on Saturday the 8th inst., at 7 o'clock in the morning, Mr. Thomas M. Sloan, in the 51st year of his age...leaving a wife and a number of children...(long eulogy).

Issue of September 21, 1849
    Departed this life at West Point, N. Y. Augustus Maverick Weyman, aged 19 years, 11 months and 25 days. (eulogy).

Issue of October 5, 1849
    Died at the residence of W. M. Ferrel (Arkansas), on the 19th August last, J. B. Ferrel, Esq., aged 46 years. He was a resident of this place for many years.

Issue of October 12, 1849
    Died at his residence in Pickens District, on the 1st inst., Maj. A. Hamilton, Sr., in the 78th year of his age...a native of Virginia, and moved to this state about 1790, selection for his abode the spot where he continued until his death, except 6 months, he spent as a soldier and capt. in the Creek Nation, during the late war. (eulogy).

Issue of November 2, 1849
    Married on the 23d ult., by Rev. Wm. G. Mullinnex, Mr. John M. Lawrence to Miss Elizabeth L. Clayton, all of Pickens.
    Married on the 24th ult., by Rev. J. S. Murray, Mr. Wm. E. Webb, of Anderson, to Miss Esther C. Lawrence, of Pickens.
    Married on the 11th ult., by Rev. W. G. Mullinnex, Mr. Wm. Douglass to Miss Sarah Ellis, all of Pickens.

Issue of November 16, 1849
    Married on the 4th inst., by Rev. W. G. Mullennix, Mr. Silas Arnold to Miss Sarah E. C. Parson, all of Pickens.
    Died, on the 9th inst., at her residence on Cane Creek, Pickens District, Mrs. Elizabeth Stribling, in the 65th year of her age...lived near 30 years where she died. She has left 10 living children, with an aged mother...(eulogy).

Issue of November 30, 1849
    Died in Pickens District, Nov. 13th, Sarah Margaret, 3rd daughter of Richard H. and L. M. Lee, aged 4 years and 8 months.

Issue of December 14, 1849
    Died, on the 14th ult., John K. Gaillard, at the residence of his father, Josias D. Gaillard, in this District, aged 23 years, 1 month and 12 days. (eulogy).
    Died, on the 6th inst., at his residence in Pickens District, Eli Fitzgerald, Esq., in the 51st year of his age, leaving a wife and four children.

Issue of December 21, 1849
    Married at Grumble Thorpe, on Tuesday, the 18th inst., by the Rev. J. L. Kennedy, Rev. J. B. Hillhouse to Miss E. L., daughter of Mr. James Steele.

Issue of December 28, 1849
    Died, in Mobile, on Tuesday Dec. 18th, Mrs. Catherine E. Lewis, wife of John W. Lewis, for many years a resident of this city.

Issue of January 11, 1850
Married on the 1st inst., by the Rev. Robert Gaines, Mr. James
Chapman to Miss Sarah Evatt, all of Pickens.
Married on the 6th inst., by the same, Mr. Peter Chapman, to Miss
Emeline Manley, all of Pickens.

Issue of January 18, 1850
Died on the 25th ult., Mr. James E. Watkins, in the 31st year of his
age...member of the Baptist Church for the last two years.

Issue of February 1, 1850
Married on the 17th ult., by Rev. W. G. Mullennix, Mr. R. M. Pickens
to Miss M. A. Burdine.
Married on the same evening, by the same, Mr. Aaron Boggs, to Miss
E. L. Stevens.
Died in Pickens District, on the 26th ult., Mr. Drury Power, in the
44th year of his age. He was born in Spartanburg, and moved to Pickens
about 20 years ago....member of the Methodist Church...left a wife and
seven children.

Issue of February 22, 1850
Married on the 7th inst., by Rev. W. G. Mullennix, Mr. G. E. McWhorter to Miss M. A. Majors.

Issue of April 5, 1850
Death of John Caldwell Calhoun...born in Abbeville District, 18 Mar
1782, his father an Irishman, his mother a native of Virginia (several
columns devoted to him).

Issue of April 12, 1850
. Married on the 4th inst., by Rev. W. G. Mullinnex, Mr. Bailey A.
Barton of Pickens to Miss Caroline Reareden of Greenville.
Died, on Tuesday the 9th April at the residence of her Brother, near
Pendleton, Maria Frances Eveleigh, only surviving daughter of the late
Judge Bee.

Issue of April 19, 1850
Married on the 14th inst., by Rev. W. G. Mullinnix, Mr. Robert A.
McWhorter, to Miss Jane E. Gilstrap, all of Pickens District.

Issue of April 26, 1850
Married on the 18th inst., at Cherry Hill, near Pendleton, by Rev.
A. H. Cornish, Mr. Thomas J. Sloan to Miss Sally Seaborn.
Also, on the 23d inst., at St. Paul's Church, by the same, Mr.
Chauncey Stevens to Miss Martha Ogier Ferrel.
Married on Wednesday morning, the 24th inst., by Rev. J. L. Kennedy,
Mr. F. E. Harrison to Miss A. Ross, all of this District.

Issue of May 3, 1850
Married on the 23d ult., by Rev. Wm. G. Mullinnex, Mr. F. M. Roberts
to Miss Nancy Jones.
Married on the 25th ult., by the same, Mr. Harmon Cox to Miss L. A.
Landers.

Issue of May 10, 1850
Married on Tuesday morning, the 31st ult., by the Rev. A. W. Ross,
Rev. J. M. Carlisle of Chester District, to Miss Elizabeth C., only
daughter of Maj. E. Sharpe, of this Village.

Issue of May 17, 1850
Died on the 28th April, near Jacksonville, Fla., James Harrison
Holland, of Pickens District.

Issue of May 31, 1850
Died, in Augusta, on the 15th inst., in the 24th year of her age,
Mary Frances, wife of Wm. J. Lomax, Esq., of Abbeville District, S. C.
A few weeks since her only child, Eliza, in her 3d year was snatched
away...(eulogy).

Issue of June 7, 1850
Death of Hon. Franklin H. Elmore. Senator from S. C., in Washington,
D. C., on the 29th ult. He was born in Laurens District. His father
was Gen. John A. Elmore, who moved to Alabama. His mother was a Saxon,
by birth. (long eulogy).
Married on Tuesday, the 4th inst., at Tusculum, near Pendleton, by
the Rev. A. H. Cornish, John Hume, Esq., to Miss Ann Mazyck Wilson.

Issue of June 28, 1850
Married in Washington city, on Thursday, June 13th by the Rev. Mr.
Pyne, Alexander F. Warley, U. S. Navy to Miss Emilie C. W., only daughter
of Capt. French Forrest, U. S. Navy.
Married on Thursday evening, the 20th inst.,by Rev. A. H. Cornish,
Mr. Henry H. Schulz, of Charleston to Miss Elizabeth G. Warley of Pendle-
ton.

Issue of July 19, 1850
Married at Bel Air, Fla., on the 27th ult., by Rev. J. H. Rice, J. N.
Whitner, Jr. of Ocala, E. F., to Miss Mary E., eldest daughter of Dr.
George Galphin.

Issue of July 26, 1850
Died, at the residence of his fahter, near this village, Frank Burt,
Jr., aged 18 years, and 4 months. (eulogy).
Died on the 19th instant, at the residence of E. S. Norris, Anderson
District, Mrs. Elenor Patterson, aged 71 years...member of the Presby-
terian Church 20 years.

Issue of August 16, 1850
Departed this life in Powder Springs, Ga., on the 29th July, Mrs.
Ann Smith, in the 35th year of her age, wife of John O. Smith, formerly
of S. C....left a husband and 5 interesting children.

Issue of August 23, 1850
Died, on the 27th June, near Pickensville, S. C., Mrs. Jane Hamilton,
aged 76 years (eulogy).

Issue of September 6, 1850
Married on the 1st inst., by the Rev. J. R. Hunnicutt, Mr. Ransom A.
O'Neal, to Mrs. Elizabeth Brewer, all of Pickens.

Issue of September 20, 1850
Died, suddenly, on the 19th July 1850, at San Antonio, Texas, John,
infant son of Samuel Augustus and Mary A. Maverick, aged 5½ months.

Issue of September 27, 1850
Married on the 17th inst., by Wm. Hubbard, Esq., Mr. A. B. Hawkins,
to Miss Catherine McDade, both of this District.
Mrs. J. C. Calhoun Jr. was bor 10 Feb 1828 and died 15 September 1850,
aged 22 years, 7 months and 5 days...daughter of a widowed mother; her
father, Rev. Jasper Adams. (eulogy).

Issue of October 4, 1850
Married on the 22d of September, by Rev. J. R. Hunnicutt, Mr. William
Whitfield to Mrs. Sillas Brady, all of Anderson District.
Died, in Macon (Geo.), on the 21st August, Mrs. Louisa C. Tillinghast,
consort of Mr. E. H. Tillinghast, in the 31st year of her age...a native
of Anderson District, and went to Georgia four years ago...from the time
she was 14, a member of the Presbyterian Church...left a husband and 5
children.

Issue of October 31, 1850
Married on the 21st inst., by Rev. J. R. Hunnicutt, Mr. Leander Osborn of Gwinnet Co., Ga., to Miss Fanny Simmons, of Pickens District.
Departed this life, on Saturday, the 5th inst., Dorothy Anna, aged
3 years, and a few months, and on Tuesday, the 8th Martha Louisa, in her
6th year, daughters of Mr. A. Gordon.

Issue of November 7, 1850
Married on Thursday, the 24th ult., by Rev. J. Scott Murray, Maj.

Willis Robinson to Miss Rebecca Griffin, all of this District.
     Married on Thursday, the 31st ult., by Rev. W. G. Mullinnex, Mr.
Latdulen Gray to Miss Martha Dowis, all of this District.

Issue of November 28, 1850
     Married on Tuesday, the 26th inst., by Rev. David Humphreys, Gen.
James Gillam of Abbeville, to Miss Louisa L. Carruth of this place.
     Died, suddenly, on the 13th inst., Mrs. Esther Steele, who was many
years an inhabitant of this town. Mrs. Steele was born June 14, 1770,
in Augusta Co., Va., baptised in the Tinkling Spring Church, and removed
with her parents to Carolina after the Revolution...member of the Presbyterian Church (eulogy).

Issue of December 19, 1850
     Married on Thursday, the 12th inst., by Rev. Edmund Anderson, Maj.
A. C. Pickens of Pickens District, to Miss Mary J. Boone of Anderson
District.
     Married on the 11th inst., by Rev. W. G. Mullennix, Mr. P. L. Gaines
to Miss Amanda Russell, both of Pickens District.
     Married on the 11th inst., by Rev. W. McWhorter, Mr. W. W. Stribling
to Miss Emily Dendy, both of Pickens District.
     Married on the 12th inst., by Rev. W. McWhorter, Mr. G. A. Taylor
of Pickens District to Miss Emily P. Cox, of Greenville District.
     Married on the 12th inst., by the same, Dr. W. Barton to Miss Louisa
A. Cox, both of Greenville District.
     Married on the 12th inst., by W. S. Grisham, Esq., Mr. Alex A. Row-
land to Miss Frances Crenshaw, both of Pickens District.

Issue of December 26, 1850
     Married on Thursday morning, the 19th inst., by Rev. J. Scott Murray,
Dr. M. B. Earle of Greenville, to Miss Harriet H., eldest daughter of
John Maxwell of that place.
     Married on the 22d inst., by Rev. D. Simmons, Mr. J. B. Edwards of
Spartanburg (formerly of Ga.), to Miss H. N. Bruce of Anderson, S. C.,
both mutes.

Issue of January 9, 1851
     Married on Tuesday, the 19th of November last, by Pev. A. Johnson,
Mr. Jas. Switzer of Lafayette, Miss., to Miss Martha T., eldest daughter
of Mr. Andrew Harris, of Anderson District. Erskine Miscellany, please
copy.
     Married on the 5th inst., by Rev. Wm. G. Mullinnex, Mr. Jas. M.
Abbott to Miss G. E. Dowis, both of Pickens District.

Issue of January 23, 1851
     Died in this village, on Sunday, the 12th inst., Mr. Toliver L. Scott,
in the 36th year of his age...left widow and orphans. (eulogy). Anderson
Gazette.
     Died at his residence, at Cumming, Forsyth Co., Ga., on Tuesday,
Dec. 17, 1850, Doctor Major J. Lewis....second son of Major Lewis, decd.,
born at Rock Mills, Anderson District, S. C. 14 June 1815, studied
medicine under Dr. Andrew P. Cater, Anderson C. H. (long eulogy). In
May 1842, he married Miss Eveline J. Lenoir, daughter of Thomas Lenoir,
Gwinnett Co., Ga., and became father of three sons and another to be
born....

Issue of January 30, 1851
     Died near Jacksonville, Benton Co., Ala., on the 4th inst., Mrs.
Permelia Burt Wright, in the 34th year of her age.

Issue of February 6, 1851
     Married in the Methodist Church, on the 2d instant, by Rev. Mr. Mc-
Gilvray, Mr. Thomas Gasaway, Jr., to Miss Clarissa McGee, both of Pickens
District.
     Died on the 25th of January, Sarah Bellotte, aged 56 years...born 17
December 1794, united with the Presbyterian Church in 1815...leaves a
husband and five children....

Issue of February 13, 1851
     Married on the 6th inst., by Rev. Wm. G. Mullinnex, Mr. James E.
Adams to Miss Martha Wright, both of Anderson District.

Issue of March 13, 1851
Married on Thursday evening, the 20th ult., by Rev. T. M. Wilkes,
Rev. L. R. L. Jennings, of Pendleton, S. C. to Miss Sallie F. Stow, of
Eatonton, Ga.

Issue of April 3, 1851
Married on Thursday evening, the 27th ult., Rev. Wm. McWhorter, Col.
E. R. Doyle to Miss Susan Dendy, both of Pickens District.

Issue of April 10, 1851
Married on the 3d inst., by Rev. Wm. G. Mullennix, Mr. John S. Newton
to Miss Mahala E. Neighbours, both of Pickens District.

Issue of May 15, 1851
Married on the 11th inst., by James F. Caradine, Esq., Mr. Simeon
Martin to Miss Charlotte Masters, both of Pickens District.

Issue of June 5, 1851
Married on the 28th ult., by Rev. W. G. Mullenix, Mr. James K. Swords
to Miss Rebecca Chapman.

Issue of June 19, 1851
Died at his residence near Selma, Dallas Co., Ala., on 28 May, Samuel B. Pickens, in the 51st year of his age...a native of this State,
but resided in Alabama 25 years...Elder in the Presbyterian Church.
Died at Huntington, L. I., on the 22d of May, in the 80th year of
her age, Mrs. Zeruah Van Wyck, wife of Abraham Van Wyck...member of the
Baptist Church.

Issue of August 21, 1851
Died at his late residence in Sumter Co., Ala., on the 28th ult.,
Richard Harris, in the 64th year of his age...a native of Abbeville
District, S. C....in the year 1836 removed to this county...for 18 years
a member of the Presbyterian Church. Sumter Democrat.

Issue of August 28, 1851
Married on Thursday evening, the 21st inst., by Wm. Hubbard, Esq.,
Mr. James C. Thompson, of Pendleton, to Miss Ann E. F. Scott, of
Charleston.
Married on the 19th inst., by Rev. J. R. Hunnicutt, Mr. Calvin Hunni-
cutt to Miss Esther Lanier, both of Pickens District.
Died at Sullivan's Island, near Charleston, on 1st August, Henry
Hamilton Schulz, aged 27 years, 5 months, and 14 days.
Died at the residence of D. Creswell, Esq., Mr. Julius Anderson, of
S. C., in the 26th year of his age...born in Pendleton, a graduate of
the College of his State in 1846, and admitted to this bar...practiced
his profession in Horry...visited this section.... Mansfield (La.)
Advertiser.

Issue of September 4, 1851
Died, in this District, on the 28th ult., Mr. William Grant, aged 90
years and 25 days. Mr. Grant held the commission of Lieutenant in a
company commanded by his father in the Revolution...he was a Blackstocks,
King's Mountain, and Cowpens...long a resident of the neighborhood where
he died.

Issue of September 11, 1851
Married on the 28th ult., by Rev. B. F. Mauldin, Mr. P. N. Acker of
Anderson District, to Miss Mary E. Garrison of Greenville District.

[The last extant issue is September 18, 1851.]

Bailey, George 76
  Hannah 29
  Isaac C. 76
  Mr. 84
  Robert 29
  Secrena C. 36
Baker, Esther 59
  Laurens F. 51
Balding, Mary 88
Baldwin, Abraham 1
  Hannah 55
  Stephen 55, 58
  Thomas 3
Ball, William Lee 18
Ballard, Mr. 37
Ballentine, Josiah J. 55
Ballew, Catherine 46
  David 57
  Robert 46
  Thomas L. 76
Banks, George W. 64
Bardine, Frances Carolina 85
  H. 85
Barker, Martha 64
Barkley, Caroline 79
  James Sr. 16
Barnes, C. W. 71
  Margaret C. 82
  Mr. 75
Barnet(t), Lucinda 34
  Parry 37
  Rebecca 42
  Samson 42
Barnwell, Mr. 42
Barr, Mary 33(2)
  Rev. 6
  Sidney 17
  Wm. 6
  Wm. H. 7, 17, 18, 65
Barrett, George 67
Barrien, William 23
Barron, Elizabeth 17
  John 17
  Polly 37
  William 37
Barry, Catherine 21
  John 23
  Nancy 21
  William H. 51
  Wm. T. 21
Barth, Matthew 60
Barton, A. 30
  Bailey 38, 81, 82
  Bailey A. 90
  Benjamin 3, 7
  Eliza 7
  Hannah 70
  Jane 3
  John 3
  Joshua 80
  Lewis 1
  Peter 30
  Phalba 82
  Ruth 30
  Sarah 14
  Squire 51
  W. 92
  William 12, 70
  William B. 65
  Wm. 46

Bat, Dr. 40
Bates, Anna 77
  Daniel 24
  Dr. 77(2)
  Sarah B. 63
  Susannah 3
Batie, Patsey 13
Batie see also Beaty and Beattie
Bay, William 38
Beattie, F. F. 45
Beattie see also Beaty and Batie
Beaty, Jane 41
  Louisa J. 61
  Miss 59
Beaty see also Batie and Beattie
Bevert, William 25
Beck, Elizabeth 10
  Isabella 15
  John 11, 15
  Mary 11
Bee, Ann F. 84
  Barnard E. 81, 84(2)
  Emma Templer 84
  Judge 90
  Marie Frances Everleigh 90
  Susan Bullein 81
Belcher, Wm. W. 30
Bell, James M. 42
  John 1
  Samuel 47
Belot, Lewis 60
Belot see also Belott(e)
Belott(e), Catherine 64
  Elijah A. 62
  John E. 71
  Peter 62
  Sarah 84, 92
Belott(e) see also Belot
Bennett, Elisha Sr. 42
  William 3
Benson, Amanda M. 48
  E. B. 37, 48, 50
  E. B. 62
  Eliza Ann 37
  Emily 26
  Eveline 39
  Harriet 9
  John P. 11
  Martha C. 50
  Mary J. 62
  Robert 39
  Thomas 9, 21, 39, 71
Berry, David 77
  Eliza S. 78
  Harriet E. 54
  Joel H. 38, 43, 58
  Louisa 58
  Martha E. 43
  Micajah F. 86
  N. 12
  William 40, 54, 78
Bertrand, Peter A. 36
Bibb, William 10
Bigbee, Oliver M. 42
Billingsley, Henry A. 73
Birch, Patsey 5
  Henry 5
Birch see also Burch
Birchfield, Elenor 10

Knox, George W. 34
  John 28, 83, 84, 85, 86
  Mary 58
  Matthew 24
  William 78
Kyle, Mrs. 25
Lamar, Millie 12
  Nathan 12
  Thomas 29
  Thomas P. 30
Lamb, Aravesta 32
Lambert, Dalcida 31
Landers, L. A. 90
Landrum, Mr. 71
Lanear, Allen 50
  Malinda 66
Lanear see also Lanier
Langston, Wm. 11
Lanier, Esther 93
Lanier see also Lanear
Lathan, Susannah 71
Latta, Alexander 10
Lattimer, Harrison 56
  Stephen S. 47
  Wiley 46
Laval, Major 5
  Rebecca 5
Law, Hugh D. 35
Lawhon, Priestley 55
  Van A. 36
Lawrence, Artemena 79
  Benjamin 2, 22
  Elisha 42
  Esther C. 89
  John M. 89
  Jos. N. 85
  Laura 42
  Margaret 2
  Martha 81
  Mary Margaret 80
Lay, C. M. 20
  Jeptha 67
Leathers, Elizabeth 37
  R. 37
Leavitt, Dorothy 31
  Mr. 74
Leboon, Mason 54
Lecroy, Hiram 51, 61
Ledbetter, Sarah 45
Lee, Ephraim 11
  John 9, 15, 19
  L. M. 89
  Richard H. 64, 89
  Samuel J. 22
  Sarah Margaret 89
  Thomas 60
  William 11
  Wm. C. 66, 72
Leeh, M. 13
Lemon, Ann 7
  Jane 9
  Martha 21
  Robert 7, 9, 21, 33
Lenoir, Evelina Jane 70
  Eveline J. 92
  Thomas 70, 92
Lesly, M. 4
Leveritt, W. 57
  Dr. 51
Leveritt see also Liverett

Lewis, A. F. 65
  Ann 11, 66
  Catherine E. 89
  Dr. 51
  Elizabeth M. 61.
  Elisha B. 46
  Frances 65
  H. T. 82
  J. 70
  James 38
  James O. 14
  Jesse 57, 87
  Jesse P. 20, 77, 88
  Joab 82
  John 7, 17
  John B. 60
  John T. 21, 27(2), 39
  J. T. 36, 38
  John W. 89
  J. W. 56, 60
  Louisa D. 49
  M. 57
  Maj. 36
  Major 14, 49, 92
  Major Sr. 54
  Melissa 36
  Nancy 59
  Nancy T. 88
  Narcissa 14
  Rachel Margaret 57
  Rebecca 15
  Richard 11, 36, 45, 68
  Robert B. 59, 72
  Robert Emile 72
  Sarah 68
  Sarah Ann 45
  Sarah M. 83
  Thomas L. 84
  William 15
Lewley, James 4
Liddell, A. 6(3)
  A. J. 20, 24, 41, 44
  Andrew J. 7, 9, 45, 87
  Andrew Sr. 41
  Daniel 3
  Eliza Jane 24
  George W. 25
  Isabella 3, 7
  James S. 60
  James Simpson 60
  Jane 60
  Joab 18
  Moses 3(2)
Liddleton, Mary 71
  Milly 71
Linn, James 14
  Jane 33
  Keziah 14
Linton, H. S. 26
  M. A. R. 30
Lively, Mr. 38
Liverett, Sarah 56
  Stephen 56
Liverett see also Leverett
Livingston, Madison C. 28
  Taliaferro 15
Lockhart, Matthew 40
Lomax, Eliza 90
  Mary Frances 90
  Wm. J. 90

McElmoyle, Elizabeth 68, 69
  William 69
  Wm. 63
McElroy, A. L. 84
  Archibald 44, 81
  John 77
  Matilda 77
  Mrs. 81
McElvany, John 1
McFall, Andrew N. 22
  John 65
  Mary Ann Frances 65
McGee, Clarissa 92
  Emeline Elizabeth 66
  Jesse S. 55
  Malinda 84
  Othneild 84
  Samuel 84
  Telitha A. 40
McGee see also Magee
McGill, Samuel 53
McGilvray, Mr. 92
McGuffin, A. 75
  Andrew 65, 71
  A. W. 85
  Elizabeth 2
  Isabella 8
  Susanna 13
  Wm. 8
McIntosh, Wm. M. 69
McKay, Wm. 6
McKinney, Ann 22
  David 34
  Eliza B. 64
  James 64, 66
  Rosamalinda 86
McLewis, C. 62
McLin, Pickens 50
McMahon, John 65
McMillan, Maria 86
McMillion, John 3
McMullin, Sarah 64
  William 64
McMurry, Wm. 54(2), 55, 63
McPhail, P. 63
  Sabina 40
McPherson, Dorcas 84
  Elizabeth 84
McPhitridge, Mary 44
McQuillen, Wm. 70
McCrea, Malcom J. 70
McWhorter, Caroline 83
  Elizabeth 78
  Isaac 58
  Robert 90
  Susannah 83
  W. G. 90
  Wm. 93
Madden, Diana 20
  Elias 16
  Nathaniel M. 83
  T. B. 78
  William 17
Mcgee, Abner 22
  Abner H. 68
  Ann Caroline 58
  Ann Melvina 71 (2)
  Elizabeth M. 71
  Eliza D. 37
  Gabriel L. 61

Magee, Jesse 59
  Jesse C. 50
  Jesse S. 58
  John 52, 58
  J. S. 37, 52
  Marilza A. 56
  Mary Elvira 56
  Michael 49
  Mr. 41
  Nancy Caroline 59
  Samuel A. 44
  T. Amanda 52(2)
  W. 39, 55(2), 56, 58, 59, 62(5), 63,
    64(2), 66(2), 68
  William 40, 43(2), 46(2), 47, 48, 51,
    58, 59
  Wm. 32, 33, 37, 40, 42, 49, 51, 52(2),
    56(2), 57, 60, 61(3), 64(2), 65,
    66, 70, 71(2)
Magee see also McGee
Major(s), Jane S. 61
  John 61
  John W. 78
  Joseph 74
  M. A. 90
  Martha Eliza 61
  William 32
Maldin, John 61
Maldin see also Mauldin
Mancel, Nancy 17
  William 17
Manigualt, Louisa M. 36
  Peter 36
Manley, Emeline 90
  Mr. 16
Manning, George 6, 50
  Louisa 50
  Mauldin R. 40
Marnock, Mary 7
Marnock see also Warnock
Martin, Charles Jr. 2
  Charles W. 63
  Eliza 43
  Elizabeth 10
  James H. 86
  Jane 86
  John 17
  Joyce Jane 2
  Martha G. 86
  Mary E. 79
  Matthew 79
  Lydia 17
  Rebecca 51
  Samuel 10
  Simeon 93
  Stephen 86
  William 76
  William D. 43
  Wm. P. 74
Mason, Andrew 3
  Benjamin 8
  Caroline 71(2)
  Elijah 79
  Mr. & Mrs. Nathan 13
Massey, Elizabeth 2
  Ephraim M. 50
  Martha Amanda 65
Master(s), Charlott 93
  Sarah 51

Place Index

CPSIA information can be obtained
at www.ICGtesting.com
Printed in the USA
FFOW03n0813310518
46861250-49094FF